LIGHT ON A DARK TRAIL

LIGHT ON A DARK TRAIL

Helen Parker

BROADMAN PRESS
Nashville, Tennessee

Dewey Decimal Classification: B
Subject heading: PARKER, HELEN // BLIND—BIOGRAPHY
Library of Congress Catalog Card Number: 82-71560
Printed in the United States of America

To my loving husband, Park, and all
the wonderful friends who helped
provide Light on a Dark Trail.

Contents

Contents

Foreword

You may be blessed with full use of your eyes. If you are, this book by Helen Parker takes you by the hand and leads you step by step through the world of a blind person. You "see" things you have never thought of before and you have an empathy—not sympathy—with a blind person. You become a knowledgeable friend of the visually handicapped. If you are a fellow church member or pastor of persons who are sightless, you will enjoy being related to them with the zest of Mrs. Parker which is a healing and loving contagion.

The wisdom of Mrs. Parker's parents, the power of the braille language, and the encouragement of the loving Christ pervade these pages. She very clearly portrays the developmental stages of her life. You meet her as an infant, as a child, as a school girl, as an adolescent, as a bride, as a wife. She gives a gentle and accurate picture of the anguish and exaltation of her life as her world expands from her family of origin to the larger family of human beings.

I have had the privilege of meeting and coming to know Helen and Park in their home. They are vital forces in their church and community. As their neighbor and friend, one who has been blessed by their generous spirits, I commend this book to you. They are among us as persons who minister and do not want to be ministered unto.

WAYNE E. OATES, Th.D.
Professor of Psychiatry and Behavioral Sciences
Director, Program in Ethics and Pastoral Counseling
University of Louisville School of Medicine
Louisville, Kentucky

Acknowledgments

I should like to express my sincere appreciation to my dear friend, Virginia Crawford, who spent hours typing and proofreading my manuscript.

I am extremely grateful to Jim Wright, picture editor of the *Louisville Times*, and others who provided the pictures for my book.

My gratitude goes to Dr. Wayne Oates, Dr. Lucien Coleman, Denise George, and Jim Cox not only for their comments about the book but for their friendship, interest, and encouragement as well.

I am especially grateful to Will Evans, superintendent of the Kentucky School for the Blind, for the time he spent updating me on the new appliances now being used to educate the visually handicapped.

I am indebted to Mary Rickert, director of the Louisville Studio of Recording for the Blind; Ned Cox, a former director of the Kentucky Bureau for the Blind; Diane Jenkins, an employee of the Kentucky Rehabilitation Center for the Blind; and the staff member of the Louisville branch Library for the Blind, for the information they supplied.

I want to thank Helen McDaniel and Harold Reagan, former classmates and friends, for the helpful suggestions they made.

I shall be eternally grateful to J. S. Parker, my husband and best friend, for his love and loyal support.

And finally I wish to thank Robert Williams, my pastor, Maurice Barnes, Jeff Conner, and Martha Wooddy, other staff members of Clifton Baptist Church in Louisville, and many other friends for their encouragement and interest in my book. The list is far too long to recognize them individually, but to each one of them I am grateful.

HELEN PARKER

Introduction

In a sense this book is my debt of gratitude to four fellow pilgrims on a dark trail who have had a profound influence on my life and on my writing. They are Helen Keller, Fanny Crosby, Louis Braille, and the blind man we meet in the Gospel of John.

Early in life Helen Keller and Fanny Crosby, two outstanding ladies, became my inspiration. Neither of them allowed their blindness to become a stumbling block.

Despite a double handicap Helen Keller devoted almost all of her adult life to improving the lot of those similarly handicapped. However, it was her indomitable spirit and positive outlook on life, reflected in one of her quotations copied from a braille magazine, that influenced and inspired me:

It has been said that life has treated me harshly; and sometimes I have complained in my heart because my pleasures of human experience have been withheld from me, but when I recollect the treasure of friendship that has been bestowed upon me I withdraw all charges against life. If much has been denied me, much, very much has been given me. So long as the memory of certain beloved friends lives in my heart I shall say life is good.

I became acquainted with Fanny Crosby through her beautiful hymns. The titles of three of them, "Blessed Assurance, Jesus Is Mine"; "To God Be the Glory"; "Praise Him! Praise Him!" have become my testimony. While still a little girl, I learned to say a poem she wrote at the age of eight:

> O what a happy soul am I!
>   Although I cannot see,
> I am resolved that in this world
>   Contented I will be;
> How many blessings I enjoy
>   That other people don't!
> To weep and sigh because I'm blind,
>   I cannot, and I won't.

Just as she endeavored to share her faith through the beautiful hymns she wrote, this book is my endeavor to share my faith through my writing.

Every blind person throughout the world, including this author, who reads and writes braille owes a debt of gratitude to Louis Braille for the system of dots that bears his name. Actually, the system is better known than the man since braille is spelled with a little "b" in most dictionaries. However, in my opinion, Louis Braille's contribution to the advancement of the blind ranks second to none.

I deeply regret that he did not receive the honor and recognition due him until 1854, two years after his death. Recognition finally came to him when Therese von Kleinet, an accomplished blind musician whom he had taught, gave a series of concerts which attracted the attention of Louis Napoleon, emperor of France. The monarch granted this talented girl an audience and ordered that the Braille system be included among the exhibits at the Paris International Exposition he was planning for the following year. Visitors to the exposition were so impressed with the Braille system that word of it soon spread to almost every country in Europe.

In his biography *Louis Braille: Windows for the Blind* J. Alvin Kugelmass, after recounting the above event, wrote:

From that point on, Braille's genius opened windows to the blind all over the world, in every climate and in every tongue wherever the tap of the cane was heard. . . .

Could he see today what he wrought, the busy workshops, the libraries and the schools and the musicians—peopled by the blind—he would bang a table with his cane and shout with excitement and pleasure. Perhaps he is.[1]

I recall the excitement that surged through me as I read aloud the ninth chapter of John from a braille Bible to some classmates. The story of a man born blind who received his sight was not new, but suddenly it had a new meaning for me. Jesus' response—"His blindness has nothing to do with his sins. . . . He is blind so that God's power might be seen at work in him"—to the disciples' question came as a revelation of why some individuals are born without sight. (See John 9:2-3, GNB.)[2]

That night alone with God I prayed, "Dear Father, let me be one of your shining lights." Hopefully *Light on a Dark Trail* is an answer to that prayer.

NOTES
1. J. Alvin Kugelmass, *Louis Braille: Windows for the Blind* (New York: Julian Messner, Division of Simon and Schuster, Inc., 1951), pp. 151-52.

2. This quotation is from the *Good News Bible,* the Bible in Today's English Version. Old Testament: Copyright © American Bible Society 1976; New Testament: Copyright © American Bible Society 1966, 1971, 1976. Used by permission.

1
Mommy, Why Can't I Tell My Puppies Apart?

"Mommy, why can't I tell my puppies apart?"

"Opal, come see my puppies," I exclaimed the minute my playmate from next door arrived at my house to play. "Mommy says I can give you one as soon as it's big enough to leave its mother."

"Oh! I want the brown and white one," Opal cried ecstatically.

"Which one is that?" I asked.

"Why, it's that one right there," she answered pointing to it. "Don't you know your colors yet?"

Her superior tone made me feel as small as the puppy I couldn't identify. Angry, perplexed, and feeling sorry for myself, I ran into the house in search of my mother. "Mommy," I demanded, "why can't I tell my puppies apart like Opal?"

This was not the first time Opal and I had observed a difference between us. Neither of us could quite comprehend why I couldn't run and play outside as freely as she and my other playmates; why I fell over a toy left in my path instead of going around it; why she sometimes had to help me locate an object which was within inches of my fingertips.

Even as a four-year-old, I was much too independent and aggressive to like some of the discoveries I was making about myself. I wanted to color. I wanted to throw and catch a ball as well as Opal, my sister Berta, and

17

other kids I played with. I longed to run as fast as they without ending up with a bump on the head or a skinned knee like my sister Daisy, who was also blind, and I usually did when we attempted to.

The realization that I couldn't distinguish one of my very own puppies from another really upset me. I wanted to know why.

My mother stopped stringing the beans she was preparing to can just long enough to lift me onto her lap. Lovingly and patiently she explained that no two people were born alike. "Each person is different," she said. "Some are short; others are tall. You are blind; Opal can see. God must have allowed this to happen to make sure mothers and dads would know exactly which little boy or girl belongs to them." I wasn't aware of the tears spilling over her eyelids when she asked, her voice trembling slightly, "Does it really matter so much that Opal can see, and you can't? You know Jesus, your dad, and I love you just the way you are."

Our conversation did more than ease the troubled mind of a little four-year-old. It sowed the seeds of faith in that little mind which have continued to grow throughout my life, helping me develop a wholesome, healthy attitude regarding my handicap. It also gave me a good self-image.

Content with the knowledge that God knew what he was about when he allowed us to be born the way we are, I jumped down from her lap. Feeling loved and accepted, I returned to my play, leaving her alone to grapple with the questions that had begun nagging my father and her when they discovered Daisy's blindness nine years ago. Why had God permitted two of their children to be born blind? Would they ever become reconciled to our handicap? Were they saying and doing the right things to help us accept and adjust to it? Then, as always, in prayer she sought the comfort, strength, and wisdom she needed to cope.

That talk was only one of several my mother and I had pertaining to my blindness while I was growing up. On other occasions I turned to her for reassurance, encouragement, and to ask why.

Another one of our talks occurred shortly after my family moved to our farm near Danville, Kentucky, from the little mountain town of Honaker, Virginia, where I was born and lived six years. I shall never forget how insecure and confined I felt in my new surroundings. How bored I was while waiting for my toys to be unpacked. How much I missed Opal, my former playmate, and a favorite aunt. How frustrated I became the day I finally mustered up enough courage to venture outside alone only to lose my way. Several minutes later Mom found me seated on a log just a few yards from our back door weeping bitterly. Dropping down beside me and putting an arm around me she inquired, "What are you doing out here all by yourself crying?"

In a single sentence without pausing once for breath I poured out my grievances. "I couldn't find the door-I don't like it here-I miss Opal-there's nothing to do. Why did we leave our nice home to come to this awful, old place?"

Mom didn't tell me how painful the decision to move had been for my father and her, nor about the sacrifice they were making in order for Daisy and me to attend a state residential school for the blind nearer our home. I didn't know until much later that they, too, felt uprooted. Dad had resigned his position as a rural mail carrier to become a farmer. All their savings had gone as a down payment on the farm where we now lived.

Through tears I couldn't see, Mom assured me it wouldn't be long until I became accustomed to my new surroundings. She predicted I'd soon know my way around and make some new friends. "Come," she said, getting to her feet and pulling me up with her, "I'll show you the big tree where your daddy is going to put up a swing for you children as soon as he has time." Together we hurried over to the tree. We then returned to the house—she to resume her work; I to seek out my sisters to tell them about our new swing.

Like the child in Robert Louis Stevenson's poem I could hardly wait to go up in that swing, up in the sky so blue. It seemed to me "the pleasantest thing/Ever a child can do!"

Mom's predictions that I'd soon grow accustomed to my new surroundings came true. I memorized the exact location of each piece of furniture in our house. Outside I discovered some landmarks as guides which enabled me to get around fairly well without assistance. The following Sunday at Sunday School I met Blanche, a girl in my class who became my best friend and a delightful playmate, and my dad found time to put up our swing.

Only one other incident occurred while we were settling in which made me long for my old, familiar surroundings. One evening after putting a record on our phonograph I started across the living room to curl up in my favorite easy chair. I had taken only a few steps when I sprawled over a low table, sending its contents flying in all directions. The crash and my sobs brought my parents on the run. Mom reached me first. Holding me close she kept asking, "Are you hurt?" My sister Berta appeared on the scene just as I managed to whimper, "I don't think so."

"Look, Mom," she cried, "Helen has broken your vase which belonged to Grandma."

Her words started me crying again. My tears this time were tears of remorse, anger, and frustration. I knew the vase I had knocked off the table in my fall was one of

Mom's most cherished possessions. It was the only thing she owned which had belonged to her deceased mother. But didn't my sister, the tattletale, realize I hadn't meant to break the vase?

Dad saved the day. "Don't worry," he said, picking up the pieces. "I can glue it together."

Mending my mother's broken vase and putting up our swing were just two of the things my father did which made him extra special. It seems only yesterday that he was cracking hickory nuts for me on a cold winter evening before an open fire. I could devour the nuts much faster than he could pick them out. Eagerly I'd gobble them up and hold out a little hand for more. "Helen," he teased, "you're as greedy as the squirrels that stole my walnuts when I was a boy."

"Oh, Daddy, please tell me about it," I begged.

The true stories of my father's boyhood delighted me even more than the ones my mother and aunts read me out of books. A favorite of mine was the story about the squirrels stealing a whole bushel of walnuts Dad had gathered and put out to dry. Through his eyes I learned that squirrels are little furry animals with long bushy tails, sharp teeth and claws, and that they get ready for winter by hiding nuts in trees or burying them in the ground.

It was my dad who let me hold a newborn lamb one spring day. It was he who helped me adjust to the arrival of my baby brother. Since I had been the baby of our family for almost eight years, I didn't like sharing the limelight with this new intruder who claimed so much of my mother's time and attention. I couldn't understand why my parents were so proud of him, or why everyone oohed and aahed so much over him, since the only thing he could do well was cry.

One evening when he was only a few days old, Dad

found me sulking in my bedroom. "Why aren't you downstairs with everyone else?" he inquired.

"Oh, Daddy," I sobbed, "Mommy likes my little brother better than she likes me."

"No, she doesn't," Dad assured me. "Your mother and I love you as much as ever. It's just that new babies require a lot of attention. They're so tiny and helpless. Besides, you're still our baby girl. Come along. It's time you got better acquainted with your brother. You'll really like him once you get to know him."

Downstairs, Dad insisted I touch his hands and feet. When he wrapped his little fingers around my forefinger, Dad exclaimed, "See, he likes you already. He's holding onto your hand and smiling at you. Isn't he sweet?"

I had to admit that he was. His little hands and feet were so soft that I liked touching his skin. I decided having a new baby around wasn't such a bad idea after all.

Once while I was small, Dad gave me a pig for a pet. My pig didn't feel like any other pets I had ever owned. His hair was coarser than that of a puppy or kitten, and he had a cute, little curly tail. I was so proud of him. It mattered not at all that my sisters kept telling me he was the runt of the litter.

"Just because he's small, doesn't mean he isn't important," I exclaimed hotly. I was smaller than they, and yet I was convinced my parents loved me as much as they loved my sisters. Quickly I pointed out to them some advantages of being small. I had more time for playing than they, and I could still sit on the laps of my parents and other adults I knew and liked. Besides, I was confident my pig would grow up into a prize hog with all the love I meant to lavish upon him.

One day I went a little too far in expressing my love. I fed my pig the cream Mom was planning to whip and serve on the strawberry shortcake she had prepared for dinner. I got whipped that day instead of the cream. My protest, "My pig is little and hungry, he likes cream, and you've always told us to be kind to animals," went unheeded.

Mom often declared that the spankings we received and the disappointments we experienced hurt Dad and her as much as they did us. Suddenly I doubted the validity of her statement concerning spankings. I certainly couldn't see any visible evidence that either of them were hurting that day.

I was still too young to perceive the anguish and heartbreak Daisy's and my blindness caused them. However, I remember well their reaction upon learning we had retinitis pigmentosia, a hereditary disorder of the retina for which there's no remedy.

The same day we were to consult an ophthalmologist, one of my friends was having a birthday party. I had been invited to the party. Naturally I wanted to go.

"Why do I have to go to the doctor when I'm not sick?" "Or why can't we go another day?" I kept asking.

Vainly Mom tried to explain to me that doctors are busy people; that finding out about my eyes was more important than going to a party; and that we had waited weeks for this appointment. "There will be other parties," she promised, "and I'm sure Blanche will tell you all about this one."

Her suggestion that Blanche tell me about it infuriated me. I was discovering that one of the things I detested most about being blind was having to rely on others to tell me about the things in which I longed to participate. "I don't want to hear about the party," I screamed, "I want to go."

Nothing Mom said appeased me. Finally in exasperation she scolded, "I'm sorry, Helen, but you've got to go to the doctor. You must learn you can't always do the things you'd rather do."

I seldom can, I thought bitterly. I kept my thoughts to myself, however. I knew from Mom's tone of voice she was becoming angry with me.

My parents were unusually quiet on the trip home. I recalled wondering if they were tired, or if Mom was still angry with me.

That night my mother put me to bed, heard my prayers, and read me a story as usual. Relieved, I decided she wasn't angry after all. But when I awoke a little later, I wasn't sure. I could hear Mom crying in the adjoining room. "Sometimes I wonder how I shall bear it," she sobbed.

"I know exactly how you feel," Dad said, blowing his nose. "But we've got to, for the children's sake."

"I realize this," Mom answered. Their voices continued, too low for me to understand everything they were saying, but I heard Mom pray. They were still talking when I fell asleep.

At breakfast Mom was her usual self. While she buttered a hot biscuit for me, I remarked, "Mommy, I thought I heard you crying last night. But I guess I was dreaming since grown-ups don't cry out loud. Do they?"

"Occasionally they do," she replied. "Mothers and daddies can hurt too."

The role of the parents of blind children is not always easy nor pleasant. So many important decisions have to be made, decisions which can affect their children's entire future. They have to decide how much and what kind of help he or she requires.

Fortunately my parents were wise enough to discover that everyone has limitations and handicaps as well as talents. Eventually they came to believe that there are greater handicaps than blindness. The failure to develop one's full potential being one of them. Therefore, their prime concern was to rear Daisy and me in a normal atmosphere, teaching us to be as independent and self-reliant as possible.

Mom taught us to bathe and dress ourselves while we were still quite small. She made us responsible for our possessions, insisting that if we had a specific place for things and kept them there we could locate them without assistance. As soon as we were old enough to do house-hold chores, we were assigned simple tasks.

One of my jobs was to wash fruit jars during canning season. Mom knew just the right psychology to get the best results. Since I was her youngest daughter and had the smallest hands, I could perform this task better than anyone else, according to her. Had she been less frugal and less industrious, her psychology might have worked; but a little girl soon tires of being called in from playing on a bright sunny day to wash jars. One day this little girl protested, "Really, Mom, I'm not sure I should have my hands in hot, soapy water so much. It might hamper my braille reading."

I knew how proud my parents were of my ability to read braille fluently. One of my teachers, bless her heart, had praised my skill to Mom.

For a minute my mother just stood there, but before I could congratulate myself on my cleverness, she broke the silence. "All right," she said, "in the future Berta can wash the jars, but you'll have to do the dusting and make the beds. It wouldn't be fair for her to do your work and hers too, would it?"

Suddenly washing jars seemed the lesser of two evils. Springing to my feet I cried, "I'll wash the jars. Maybe it won't hurt my hands after all. Besides, Berta can't get her hands inside them."

That experience taught me three valuable lessons that

have helped me live with blindness. I learned I could not use my handicap to manipulate my mother or to avoid a task I disliked. I also learned not to expect preferential treatment because of my blindness.

My parents wanted Daisy and me to merit the admiration and esteem we received from others. Once an acquaintance of my mother's complimented me for some minor achievement in my sister Berta's presence. Turning to Mom she inquired, "Aren't you proud of Helen?"

"Many times I've been proud of all my children," Mom answered.

My parents tried not to show partiality. They loved each of their children, and we were all aware of it. They never allowed Daisy and me to make unnecessary demands on our sister and little brother.

I didn't realize until I was much older and had had an opportunity to meet and observe some other blind children how wise my parents really were. I distinctly remember one teenage student coming to school who had never been taught to dress himself or to eat with a fork, even though his parents loved him dearly. I recall another student who had temper tantrums when she didn't get her way. These individuals were never well adjusted.

I'm not saying that my parents always did all the right things, but I'm glad they were not afraid to experiment in order to find out what I could or couldn't do. I'm glad they refused to do for me and to let others do the things I was competent to do for myself.

I shall be eternally grateful to them for their love and understanding and for some of the things we learned together that have given me a positive outlook on life, making it easier for me to live with blindness.

2
Oh, I've Got Good Ears!

Overjoyed at having won a game at my cousin's birthday party I accepted the beautifully wrapped package containing my prize. I could hardly wait to see what lay beneath those fancy wrappings. Eagerly, I tore them away. My prize was a lovely toy, china tea set, just perfect for a doll's tea party. As I examined each miniature piece, an exact replica of my mother's tea set, I was anticipating many happy hours of play.

The game I had just won was a listening game in which the players were required to answer questions based on a funny story that my aunt read to us. Lucky me! I had answered the most questions correctly.

"How in the world did you know the answers to all those questions?" the girl beside me inquired.

"Oh, I've got good ears!" I boasted.

Every day of my life I was growing more and more aware how dependent a person without sight is on his remaining senses, especially hearing and touch. Already my ears and fingertips had become my eyes in perceiving the world around me. Already my very good ears were helping me adapt to my surroundings. Through my ears, I was discovering I lived and moved in a world of sound. By listening I began to learn many new and interesting things which have enriched my life.

One of my first discoveries was that no two people talk exactly alike just as no two people look exactly alike. Just as a sighted individual puts a name with a face, I began to put names with voices until I could recognize several friends and acquaintances as well as family members the moment I heard them speak.

Frequently I surprised a visitor by greeting him before he had an opportunity to speak to me. "How did you know I was around?" he usually asked.

Laughing, I'd reply, "Oh, I've got good ears! I heard you talking," or "I heard you when you arrived." If we were expecting guests, I would sometimes listen for their footsteps or some other sound that marked their arrival.

I seldom confused one person with another unless the person speaking deliberately changed his voice. This always annoyed me since a person's voice was generally my only means of identifying him.

"How did he expect me to know him?" I complained to my mother. "I'll bet he wouldn't know me if I wore a mask."

Mom would explain that it was just his way of teasing me. "Although people are sometimes thoughtless, the majority of them are basically kind," she assured me. "Try to accept them the way they are."

I didn't know until much later that it had not always been easy for Mom to accept people the way they were. I didn't know how difficult it had been for her to overcome her resentment when curious bystanders had stared at my sister and me or had asked questions and made tactless remarks about our blindness.

I have never learned to like it when someone attempts to fool me by changing his voice. However, it no longer upsets me; nor do I consider him unkind.

By listening, I discovered I could detect a person's mood from the tone of his or her voice. "Mom is cross today," I'd remark to my sisters. Or, "You must be tired," I'd say to a friend. Usually I was right.

My good ears helped me not only to know who people were, but where they were, and occasionally what they were doing. The whirr of Mom's eggbeater signified she was in the kitchen mixing up one of her good home-baked desserts. The ring of Dad's axe against a log indicated he was in the woodlot chopping wood for our fireplace. Certain inanimate objects around our house had a distinct sound of their own. For example, our tea kettle singing, and our mantle clock ticking away the hours were familiar sounds. These objects were soon like old friends.

As children, one of the highlights of our day was Dad's return home from his job as a rural mail carrier. At that time Dad delivered the mail on horseback. Instead of watching for his appearance like my sister Berta, Daisy and I would listen for the first "clop, clop" of his horse's hooves on the highway as it trotted homeward. Dad usually had a sucker, crackerjacks, or some small treat for us.

My parents could not afford to buy us expensive presents while we were growing up, but from time to time we received small surprises. My favorite treat was crackerjacks. In addition to the goodies inside the box there was a prize. The prizes I liked best were the ones that made some kind of noise.

I preferred toys that appealed to my senses of hearing and touch instead of the brightly colored ones that appeal to children with normal vision. I recall how surprised my parents were the Christmas I asked Santa Claus to please bring me a drum, and how delighted I was with my first "mama" doll. My sister Berta declared she was not as pretty as my other dolls. Nevertheless, of all my dolls she continued to be my favorite.

Early in life I learned to recognize all our farm animals and some of the birds that nested nearby by their cries.

Like the average preschooler I'd proudly tell you that a cow says "moo," a sheep "baa," and a cat "meow." I knew that a dove coos, a quail calls "bobwhite," and a hen makes a variety of different sounds. She cackles when laying an egg, clucks to her baby chicks, and squawks when in danger of being attacked by an enemy.

In addition to my good ears I possessed an inquring mind. While quite small, I began asking questions about a myriad of subjects. "What does a rainbow look like?" "What month comes after January?" and "What makes our clock strike the hour?" were typical questions. I was certainly not one of those children content to be seen and not heard. I wanted to be heard and to hear. There was so much to hear and to learn, and I knew so little. I listened attentively to the conversations of adults, hoping to glean some bits of information from their discussions. I'm sure that I sometimes heard remarks I was not intended to hear, and occasionally I made false assumptions from the things I heard.

I recall Mom informing us one morning at breakfast that a varmint had gotten into our chickens. Later that day when a neighbor called, Mom began telling her about it. "Do you suppose it was a fox?" our visitor inquired.

"Oh, no, it was a varmint," I cried. I couldn't understand why everyone was laughing until, putting an arm around me, my mother explained, "Honey, all animals that prey on chickens are varmints."

Anyone who did explain something to me, answer my questions, or read me a storybook was my friend. Listening to stories was a favorite childhood pastime of mine. I enjoyed fairy tales, adventure stories, how-to stories, and the Bible stories I heard. Our bedtime stories were frequently Bible stories. My favorite Bible story was the one about the baby Moses' rescue and adoption by an Egyptian princess. Another story I liked was the one about David's victory over the giant Goliath; that Philistine giant delighted me as much as the giant in "Jack and the Beanstalk."

Listening to those Bible stories at home and attending Sunday School helped me learn about the love, grace, and power of God. Throughout life, my ears have contributed to my Christian growth as I've listened to the teaching and preaching of God's Word. Beautiful sacred music has always had the power to inspire me.

My good ears proved extremely helpful once I started to school. A blind student relies on his ears for much of his knowledge. A teacher of blind children cannot use the visual aids employed by a teacher of sighted pupils. Much of the teaching at the Kentucky School for the Blind, the school I attended, was done orally.

In the 1930s, at the time I entered college, only print textbooks were available. Once more my good ears afforded a solution to my problem. I discovered I could prepare my assignments by listening to another student read them aloud.

As I grew older, I became aware I had what scientists term "facial vision." Contrary to terminology, facial vision has nothing whatever to do with one's vision. It is a built-in sonar system especially discernible in bats. Facial vision is the ability to perceive nearby objects such as a parked car or a telephone pole even though they are not visible to the eye. It is a definite asset to a person traveling alone without sight. As he moves along he listens for the sound waves that bounce off the objects he encounters.

Everyone has some facial vision. However, those with normal sight are usually unaware of it and seldom develop it since they are not dependent on it. A keen sense of hearing and acute concentration on one's environment are essential in the development of facial vision.

Not all of the blind have it to the same degree.

A person traveling alone without sight learns to depend on his ears to warn him of the approach of an oncoming vehicle. In order to cross a street safely he listens to the flow of traffic and the movement of other pedestrians. In certain areas of some cities buzzer traffic lights controlled by a push button have been installed at strategic crossings to aid the blind. It is not feasible to place these lights at all crossings since it would tie up traffic.

Not all sounds aid the blind traveler. A brisk wind, a jet plane flying overhead, or any noise which drowns out the movement of traffic hampers his progress in getting around.

Occasionally the visually impaired misinterprets a sound as the following anecdote illustrates. One day while my husband and I were walking down the street, a dog ran toward us barking furiously. Swinging his cane in its direction, my husband shouted, "Get!" Assuming the dog had gone, we proceeded on our way. We had taken only a few steps when we heard a noise. "That dog is back," I cried. Once more my husband swung his cane and shouted, "Get!" Imagine our surprise and chagrin when a neighbor spoke to us. The dog had not returned. The sound we heard was our neighbor walking in the fallen leaves.

In recent years several aids and appliances involving hearing which benefit the blind have become available. One of the most important is the talking book. Talking books and talking-book machines, property of the Library of Congress, can be obtained free by the blind and physically handicapped unable to read. The recipient is allowed to keep the machine, which resembles a phonograph, as long as he or she needs it. A state agency supplies him with a machine. He then borrows the books he wishes to read from a regional or branch library for the blind just as a sighted individual borrows reading material from his local library. Several current periodicals and books on every subject including many of the best-sellers are available. One advantage of talking books is their high quality. The recording is done in studios resembling commercial studios. The books are read by professional speakers such as radio announcers and actors.

Another advantage of the talking book over a braille book is that one can read while doing her housework or dressing to go out.

The talking book is a real boon for adults losing their sight in later life who either cannot or do not wish to learn braille but who still enjoy reading.

Another aid finding its way into many homes is a talking clock which can be purchased for around $58.00.

This little battery-operated timepiece is compact enough to fit into one's purse or pocket. These are some of the features my husband and I like about our talking clock. We can tell the correct time any hour of the day or night by simply pressing a button. Our clock can be set to announce the time at half-hour intervals or at one-minute intervals over a ten-minute period. Our talking clock serves as our alarm clock.

Recently one of my friends was so delighted with her new talking clock that she decided to take it to church to show to some of her friends. She forgot it was set to announce the time every half hour. She and all those sitting near her were startled to hear the words "It's 11:30 AM" right in the middle of the minister's sermon.

Afterwards when she related the story, she commented, "Evidently my pastor did not hear my little man an-

nounce the time since he kept on preaching as if nothing
had happened."

For years my ears have provided most of my recreation.
I spend much of my leisuretime listening to talking
books, good music, the radio, and television. I also like to
engage in chitchat with friends. My husband, a sports
fan, enjoys listening to all kinds of sports events on radio
and television. They are much easier to follow on radio,
however.

My good ears enable me to be a more efficient homemaker. In my kitchen by listening, I know when to turn
the heat down under the food I am cooking or when it is
in danger of boiling dry. By listening to my automatic
washer, I know when to add fabric softener to my laundry.

Ever since I began teaching Sunday School approximately thirty years ago, I have been letting my ears do
the walking for me by using the telephone to contact
prospects, shut-ins, and the absentees in my class.

My ears have helped me in still another way. I am sure
I would never have attained some of my goals had it not
been for the words of encouragement, praise, and reassurance I heard spoken by understanding parents, interested teachers, a loving husband, and wonderful friends.
The words of my parents, "You can do it," often spurred
me on to attempt new and different things. The encouragement of a teacher influenced my decision to attend
college. I've grown to depend on my husband's loyal
support in all my endeavors. It was the suggestion of
another writer and wonderful friend, Dr. Lucien Coleman, that caused me to submit my first article to *Outreach*, a Southern Baptist periodical.

With every passing day I thank God for my good ears
which enable me to hear the songs of birds in spring, my
husband whistling, popcorn popping, my editor calling

me long distance to tell me my book was approved, beautiful music, and the voice of a Christian lifted in prayer. These are my favorite sounds.

Undoubtedly my good ears and sensitive fingertips have played a prominent part in helping me overcome my handicap. As soon as I began to discover how much information lay at my fingertips, I became as eager to touch as I had been to hear. My inquisitive fingers were soon giving me an idea of the size, shape, and texture of the things around me.

With my intense desire to know what things were like, is it any wonder I got upset when Mom reprimanded, "Honey, don't touch"?

Is it any wonder I would always protest, "But Mommy, I want to see"?

Usually my mother would relent. "All right," she would concede, "you may see, but touch lightly."

When a blind person expresses the desire to see something, he really wants to touch it. Since this is his means of perceiving things, he refers to it as seeing.

At the same time I began to recognize people and animals by sound I started to identify the parts of my body, my toys, my wearing apparel, household furnishings, and other familiar objects by touch.

I grew up on a farm where we had our own vegetable garden and orchard. I liked to accompany my mother to gather the fresh fruits and vegetables for our table. On these trips I learned to recognize a wide assortment of vegetables and fruits, to tell when vegetables were ready to be picked, and to distinguish ripe fruit from green.

While growing up I had several different animals as pets. One of my favorites was a dear little kitten named Softy. I liked to stroke Softy and other animals covered with fur.

Over the years my sensitive fingertips have continued to keep me informed. I regard them as my ten most faithful helpers.

Throughout life, my senses of hearing, touch, smell, and taste have served me well. Despite my blindness they have made me aware of the wonder of creation and of how good God, my creator, has been to supply me with everything I need to live a rich, full life.

3
Six Magic Dots

"I'm sorry I don't have time to read you a story tonight," Mom remarked on entering our bedroom, "but before I hear your prayers, I've something to tell Berta and Helen."

Immediately, I began wracking my brain to think if my sister and I had done anything today to cause my mother's disapproval. However, instead of scolding us she continued, "You know your Daddy and I are taking Daisy to school tomorrow. We'll be gone a week since we plan to stay with her a few days. I want you to be good girls while we're away. Your Aunt Ida and Virgie will look after you." Virgie was a foster sister who had come to live with us when Daisy was a baby.

Of course I had known about my parent's plans to take Daisy to the state residential school for the blind in Staunton, Virginia. However, I had not known that it was a two-day journey by train from our home. When the realization that my parents would be gone for several days dawned on me, I didn't like the idea at all since I had never been separated from them for more than a day.

"Mommy, let me go with you," I begged. "I want to go to school too."

"You're too little," Berta observed. "Three-year-old girls don't go to school."

"Well, I could go," I answered hotly. "I know as much as you. I can spell my name and count to ten."

"Children, stop fussing," Mom reprimanded. Then turning to me she added, "Honey, I can't take you with me, but if you're a good girl while I'm away I'll bring you a surprise."

Visions of the surprise Mom would bring me filled my mind that night as I drifted off to sleep.

My parents liked the Virginia School for the Blind well enough. What they disliked was the long, tiresome journey with layovers to and from Staunton and being separated from Daisy from September until June. Those inconveniences aroused their desire to move nearer a state institution for the blind.

In the meantime, some of our relatives had moved to a little town near Danville, Kentucky. The summer I was five we accepted an invitation to visit them. It was on this visit that we learned the Kentucky School for the Blind in Louisville was only a three-hour trip by train from Danville.

At first sight my parents had fallen in love with the beautiful, fertile farmland of central Kentucky. When they heard that a farm they had seen and liked was for sale, Mom was convinced it was God's leading. For some time she had been seeking divine guidance regarding their decision to move.

I didn't enter school at the age of six because plans were under way for us to come to Kentucky the following January. At first I was disappointed. I was so eager to learn, and I had been looking forward to going away with my sister Daisy whom I adored.

I still recall how excited I was the summer prior to my enrollment at the Kentucky School for the Blind. I remember how I chattered on and on about going to school, my new wardrobe, and the trunk my parents had purchased for me to take with me. Having my own trunk made me feel quite grown-up and important.

Eventually the day arrived for me to leave for the institution I'd be attending the next twelve years. When the time finally came to say good-bye to those I loved, I began to have a few misgivings. Perhaps going away to school was not as glamorous as I had imagined. From September until June was a long time to be absent from home. Suppose my family forgot me or stopped loving me while I was gone.

My parents assured me my fears were groundless. They reminded me they had not forgotten Daisy nor stopped loving her. They promised to write to me often and to visit me whenever they could.

They kept their promise to write often. Letters from them usually arrived on Tuesdays and Fridays. Sometimes hearing about my friends, my pets, and their various activities made me a little homesick. I slept with their letters under my pillow.

Frequently, Daisy and I received boxes from home. Our packages usually contained fudge, homemade cookies, and jelly made from fruit on our farm. Having such goodies to share with classmates undoubtedly enhanced my popularity.

I liked almost all of my schoolmates who came from all over the state and from a diversity of backgrounds. However, the differences between some fellow students and myself came as somewhat of a shock to me since my friends at home and I were from similar backgrounds. I had not been at school long when I discovered that some of the pupils were educable or trainable while others had learning disabilities. Some were well behaved; others were disobedient and rebellious. I soon became aware that the only thing many of us had in common was our blindness.

At the time I entered school the building was well known throughout Kentucky for its fine architecture.

Actually, it was one of thirteen landmarks in the entire country. It was a huge, five-story, stone-and-brick structure, housing the classrooms, dormitories, food center, and laundry.

I slept in a dormitory with nine other girls and a house mother who looked after us. Although Daisy and I were not in the same dormitory, we managed to see each other every day.

I was barely seven and weighed only thirty-five pounds when I started to school. Since I was the smallest girl there, I soon became just about everybody's pet.

I loved school from the opening day. In the first grade we learned reading, writing, and arithmetic. Actually, our curriculum was similar to that of the public school except our textbooks were in braille—a dot system invented in 1824 by Louis Braille, a blind Frenchman who taught at a school in Paris. The first braille code was published in 1829. This code is now used universally in the production of books for the blind.

Braille is built around a rectangular cell consisting of six dots numbered from top to bottom. The three dots on the left are 1, 2, and 3; those on the right are 4, 5, and 6. The letters of the alphabet and the punctuation marks are a combination of one or more dots. For example, *a* is dot *1*; *b* dots *1* and *2*; a period dots 2, 5, and 6; a hyphen dots 3 and 6. The numbers are the first ten letters of the alphabet preceded by a number sign dots 3, 4, 5, and 6. To increase the speed of a braille reader single letters represent words. The letter *b* standing alone is but, the letter *c* can, and so on. It is possible to make sixty-three different symbols from these six dots—hence their magic power. Some symbols represent both whole and part-word signs. For example, the word *for* is dots 1, 2, 3, 4, 5, and 6. The word *forest* is written *for* sign, the letter *e* dots 1 and 5, and the *st* sign dots 3 and 4. The blind learn to recognize these symbols by touch as they slide their fingertips across a page from left to right. Some of the visually impaired employ both hands to read braille. I use only the forefinger on my right hand. I can read rapidly with this finger but I can hardly distinguish one letter from another with my other fingers since I have not developed their sense of touch.

Reading was my favorite subject in the first grade. I had an advantage over the other kids because I already knew some of my letters. It was not long until I could read braille fluently. Soon I was reading aloud to classmates, a practice I continued throughout school. Once I had mastered braille I became an avid reader. From then on I was never without a storybook. From then on I began to regard braille as six magic dots, six magic dots which provided much light on a dark trail. Due to their magic power a whole new world started coming alive for me. I discovered I could see many things I would otherwise have missed. I could get a good mental picture of places near and far.

Those six magic dots soon became my passport to distant lands, allowing me to have all sorts of exciting adventures and to enjoy a wide variety of different experiences. Through them, I made friends with such charming people as Aladdin with his wonderful lamp, Tom Sawyer, Heidi, and the March sisters in *Little Women*. These characters became as real to me as my living playmates as I laughed with them, wept with them, and shared with them in their adventures. Later on I met Hamlet, David Copperfield, Scarlet O'Hara, and scores of other fascinating characters. I shall always treasure the happy hours I spent in their company.

The school had a small library from which I could borrow books. During vacation I obtained reading matter from a regional library for the blind.

Frequently I took a book to bed with me at night. Reading a storybook during study period and in bed got me in trouble more often than anything else.

Like average school kids we enjoyed playing practical jokes on our friends. I shall never forget an occasion when I was the butt of a joke.

One morning I overslept after having stayed awake to finish an exciting mystery story. Hurriedly I dressed and made my bed in order not to be late for breakfast. Sometime during the morning I remembered my book still at the foot of my bed. Alas! When I returned to the dormitory to retrieve it, it was gone. Naturally I assumed the maid who cleaned our room had taken it. I spent a miserable day expecting to be summoned to the office any minute. When I crawled into bed that night my toe touched something hard, my missing book. One of my roommates had found it and hidden it from me.

Those six magic dots enabled me to master some new skills such as braille writing. Along with our readers the first-grade pupils received a slate and stylus, the necessary tools to write braille. A slate consists of a hinged metal guide with four rows of cells. The paper fits into this guide which is moved along until the page is filled. The dots are punched with the stylus which resembles an awl.

Those six magic dots satisfied my quest for knowledge in a variety of subjects such as languages, music, mathematics, and science. In addition to the regular texts our mathematics, science, and geography books contained embossed drawings. To further assist us in the study of geography we used large wooden maps of the countries resembling jigsaw puzzles. I vividly recall the map of Kentucky which consisted of 120 pieces, one for each county. This particular map had been hand carved by a former superintendent of the school. He had built up the wood to show the mountains, indentations marked the rivers, tacks represented the county seats, a larger tack the state capitol.

All our learning appliances were the property of the school.

An aid to the study of physiology was a skeleton whom we nicknamed Alec. So many rumors, some of them fairly wild, were circulated about his identity that at first I was reluctant to touch those dry bones. However, my intense curiosity about my own bones helped me overcome my fear and all of old Alec, whatever his past.

With the aid of those six magic dots I gained my first recognition as a writer. The year I was in the second grade the school sponsored a writing contest for the elementary pupils. The child submitting the best short story about his pet would receive a braille book titled *Dr. Gander*, stories about a goose, as a prize. From the minute I heard about the contest I coveted that prize. Imagine having a book of one's very own! As yet, I didn't own any books since braille books were too expensive for me to buy.

Immediately I began work on my story. I decided to write about my collie dog whom I had insisted on naming Collie even though my sisters had laughed at me and said it was not a suitable name. I enjoyed writing about Collie. In my opinion she was no ordinary pet. She was my playmate and friend, I her special charge.

When I sat down to write, I suddenly realized I couldn't spell Collie, and as yet I didn't know how to look up words in a dictionary. I solved my problem by calling my dog Happy, a word I knew how to spell. The name seemed appropriate for she was so playful, and I was certainly being original. One of the rules of the contest was that our stories must be original.

Shortly after I had submitted my story, I met the

superintendent, one of the judges, in the hall. "Helen," he inquired, "do you really have a dog named Happy?"

"No, sir," I replied truthfully, "my dog's name is Collie, but since I couldn't spell Collie, I called her Happy. I didn't want to have any misspelled words in my story."

The night I was awarded the prize the superintendent related the above incident. I have sometimes wondered whether my story or the truth won me the prize and all the applause I received that night.

I eventually learned to spell Collie and many, many other words with the help of six magic dots.

Near the end of each school year we were tested in spelling in a spelling match between the boys and girls. The competition was as keen as that of any sports event. The girls could have won easily had it not been for one boy in my class. All during high school until our senior year he was the champion, I the runner-up. That year, however, I managed to win. The girls were jubilant over the victory. They carried me around the auditorium cheering lustily. I couldn't have received more acclaim had I been a star football player.

As well as our academic courses, the school offered classes in typing, physical education, and chorus. Students desiring to learn to play piano could take music lessons. The boys received vocational training in piano tuning, chair caning, and band, while the girls studied home economics and crafts.

Our day began with the ringing of the rising bell at 6:30 AM. A bell summoned us to breakfast at seven. The chapel bell rang at eight. All students were required to attend chapel. Our school day was divided into 45-minute periods with a midmorning recess. A bell at the end of each period sent us scurrying to our next class. The lunch bell rang at noon; the dinner bell at 5 PM. A supervised study period was scheduled from 6:30 until 7:30 PM, followed by an hour-long reading period, during which a teacher read aloud to us. Our day ended with the retirement bell at 9 PM.

During our vacant periods we could study, practice, or play. Our playgrounds were equipped with swings, see-saws, a sliding board, and a bandstand. There was a large play area with enough space to jump a rope, bounce a ball, or play such childhood games as London bridge. In the fall we romped joyfully in the leaves. When it snowed we got out the sleds and went sleigh riding. A steep hill on the campus afforded an ideal spot for coasting. In order to avoid mishaps a partial sighted student and a blind student teamed up and coasted together.

Scouting was one of the most popular extracurricular activities. As a girl scout, I worked hard to pass the tests and to obtain as many merit badges as possible. But the part of scouting I liked best were the hikes, sing-alongs around a camp fire, and the other outings.

A state residential school for the blind, like any other boarding school, is responsible for the well-being of its pupils. Our school had an infirmary to care for patients who became ill. A seamstress was employed to sort and mend our clothes. Maids waited on us at the table and cleaned the building. We were required to make our beds and to keep our lockers in order. A barber came to the school periodically to cut our hair. A teacher read our mail and wrote cards and letters home for us until we learned to type well enough to take care of our own correspondence.

A brief excerpt of the first letter I ever typed follows:

DEAR MOM AND DAD:
I'm typing this letter myself . . .

Last week some of us had the opportunity to hear Helen Keller, the famous deaf-blind lady I admire so much, speak.

I had intended to write deaf but instead of the *f* I had struck the *d* which is next to the *f* on the typewriter. That was not the only error in my letter, but it was one neither my parents nor I ever forgot.

I have many fond memories of the time I spent at the Kentucky School for the Blind. I still recall the hymn sings each Sunday evening when we memorized the words to the beautiful old songs we sang during chapel. I remember the good times we had at the parties the teachers planned to commemorate special days such as Halloween, Christmas, and Valentine.

Another occasion we looked forward to was the candy store twice a week when we were allowed to purchase our favorite candy bar. Other events I enjoyed were the concerts we attended, a trip downtown at Christmastime, and an outing at an amusement park in the spring. Occasionally a group of entertainers came to the school to present a program. From time to time we also presented programs to which the public was invited.

When the time eventually came for me to graduate from high school, I really had mixed emotions. I hated leaving friends I might never see again, and yet I felt glad and proud to have reached a milestone in life. I was looking forward to college if I could possibly make the necessary arrangements to go.

At college the following September I continued to rely on my six magic dots. My clear, concise braille notes proved invaluable not only to me but to fellow students who soon began expressing the desire to study with me before a test.

I don't know why but at first I felt self-conscious about

writing braille in class. However, I knew that if I were to succeed in college I had to overcome my feelings. One day in the student lounge I had what I considered a brainstorm. Opening my purse I took out my slate and began to write braille. After writing a few words, I commented to a nearby student, "I bet you wonder what I'm doing."

"I suppose you're writing braille," she replied timidly.

"Would you like for me to write your name?" I inquired.

"Please do," she cried, introducing herself.

"Would you mind writing my name for me?" someone else asked.

"Not at all," I answered.

I spent the remainder of that period writing the names of classmates. I wrote and passed out so many names I began to feel like a celebrity handing out autographs. Those six magic dots had served as an icebreaker.

Shortly after my graduation from college, I accepted a position as a braille proofreader for the American Printing House for the Blind in Louisville, a position I could never have filled had it not been for six magic dots. Coming back to Louisville to work was like returning home, so many of my friends were there.

Throughout the years six magic dots have helped me in countless ways. My household gadgets marked in braille and my braille recipes make it possible for me to serve more appetizing meals and to be a more efficient homemaker. Having the telephone number of my doctor, plumber, beautician, and others I need to contact written in braille saves me time. My braille watch enables me to be punctual for my appointments. *Reader's Digest* and other current periodicals available in braille keep me abreast of what is going on in the world. My braille scrabble board, bingo game, and playing cards increase my popularity with both blind and sighted friends.

Those six magic dots have undoubtedly opened some

doors for me that might otherwise have remained closed. My braille Bible and the Sunday School lessons I receive have made it possible for me to teach Sunday School for the past thirty years. My Bible also provides the background material essential for the writing I have been doing for Christian periodicals since 1975. The first draft of my manuscripts including this book are written in braille.

I shudder to think how dull and empty my life would have been without six magic dots. Truly I consider them one of my greatest blessings.

4
Blind Dates

One of my self-appointed tasks the summer I was fifteen was going for the mail. Our mailbox, which was situated approximately 100 yards from our house at the end of a lane, was one of the few places I could go by myself. The mail arrived around eleven o'clock. Every morning at about five minutes before eleven I'd set off for the mailbox since that was the summer I began receiving love letters.

I still recall the day my first letter from a boy arrived. "You're the most popular member of your family," our mailman, a neighbor, observed handing me the daily paper, a sale catalog, and two braille letters.

The first letter I opened was from a boy in my class. In my excitement I completely forgot about the other one until my sister Berta reminded me of it some time later.

"Daisy, you'll never guess who I received a letter from today," I cried. "I've no idea. Who?" she asked.

"Seborn Wilhoit," I answered. "He says he has admired me ever since we were in grade school. He wants to correspond with me if I'm interested."

"Are you interested?" my mother wanted to know.

"Oh, yes," I replied truthfully. "Seborn is the nicest boy at school. Mom, you should hear him play the piano and organ. He's really talented." The preceding year I had often listened to him practicing the organ. Many times I had longed to tell him how much I enjoyed his music.

Although not a musician myself, I was a music lover.

Once Seborn and I decided to correspond I could hardly wait to tell my chums, who were dating, that I now had a boyfriend too.

Over the next ten years we must have written each other hundreds of letters. We continued to correspond until I became engaged. However, we had relatively few dates since we lived in different towns and since the Kentucky School for the Blind prohibited dating among its pupils.

At the time we were students there the school was coeducational in name only. The boys and girls were completely segregated. The girls occupied the east side of the building; the boys the west. We even had separate playgrounds. In the central dining room, auditorium, and classrooms we shared, we were always seated on opposite sides of the room. Nevertheless, by the time we were in our teens almost all of us had become interested in members of the opposite sex. Like average teenage girls my roommates and I enjoyed talking about the boys and speculating on love and marriage since the blind possess the same urges, desires, and aspirations as their sighted peers.

The year I was sixteen a newly appointed superintendent of the school began allowing us to attend the church of our choice. Since I was a Baptist, I chose Clifton, a local Baptist church within walking distance of the school. On Sundays some of the sighted members came to walk to and from church with us. In the sanctuary we could sit wherever we wished. The students from the school usually paired off and sat together. To church was the only place we were permitted to go without a chaperon. We could never talk to each other as much as we desired, but I regret to say that sometimes I talked during the service more than I should have.

That year I kept a diary. A typical entry follows:

Sunday, September 12—
We are going out to church this year. I am attending
Clifton. The girls in the Sunday School class all seem
very nice. _____ and I sat together, held hands, and
exchanged notes at church today. I wonder if I'm falling in
love.

I never wrote Seborn's name in my diary nor in our
notes. Should they fall into the wrong hands, I didn't
want to disclose his identity.

One Sunday during the organ prelude I admitted to
Seborn that I listened to him practice the organ every
night.

"I wish I could serenade you with love songs," he
commented, "but I know I couldn't get by with it. However, I could play something like 'Brahms Lullabye.' No
one would ever suspect that was my way of saying 'good
night, sweetheart' to you." From then on he played
"Brahms Lullabye," our special song, every night.

At church was not the only time or place where we
exchanged notes. We devised other means, some of them
fairly ingenious, to write to each other. For example,
some of the classrooms were located on the girl's side of
the building; others on the boy's side. Frequently we left
notes in the desks we occupied. At other times we'd insert
a note in a library book we were returning. The person to
whom it was written would check that book out immediately. The students who lived in Louisville and went
home for the weekend would either mail letters for us or
would bring us letters which had been sent to their
addresses.

Occasionally a couple would risk expulsion and slip out
to meet each other. I was never that bold. I didn't dare do

anything to jeopardize my opportunity to obtain an education. Besides, I knew my parents would not approve. Fortunately, none of the boys I liked ever suggested it.

Incidentally Seborn was not the only boy interested in me during high school. The last years I was there Ernie Hooker, a new student losing his sight, and I liked each other. Since he had travel vision, he used to visit me at home during vacation.

Regardless of who Seborn or I dated we always remained fond of each other. He seemed pleased when he learned I was planning to attend the University of Kentucky in Lexington, his hometown. "If you do come to Lexington, there's no reason why we can't go steady," he remarked.

We were both disappointed when my plans to go to the university did not materialize. Circumstances beyond my control compelled me to live at home and attend Centre College in Danville.

I seldom dated anyone at college. I liked to think it was because I didn't live on campus where I could have participated in more of the social functions, becoming better acquainted with more of the male students; or that things might have been different had I been a little more secure and a little less particular. As reluctant as I was to admit it there was simply no way that I, a totally blind girl, could date the students I really admired. I wanted the young men I went out with to be attractive and intelligent.

Once when I made that statement to a sighted friend she inquired, "How can you tell whether a person is attractive or not?"

"I realize I am not as conscious of one's physical appearance as you are," I responded, "but certain characteristics such as a pleasant voice and a pleasing personality make an individual attractive to me. I also admire people who are quick-witted, fun loving, and kind."

Despite the fact that I rarely dated during college I had too many interests and outlets to be lonely, bored, or unhappy. I was well liked by fellow students who were always kind and helpful even though I seldom dated any of them. I studied hard in order to make good grades, and I worked in my local church teaching a Sunday School class of high school girls. One year while at college, I taught a young man, who had just lost his sight, to read braille. I'm almost positive I could have gone with him had I desired. Since he didn't appeal to me, I discouraged his advances—although I felt sorry for him and truly enjoyed helping him learn braille. I saw Seborn and Ernie occasionally and continued to correspond with them regularly.

As soon as I returned to Louisville to work after graduation, some of the young men I had known in high school began calling me and inviting me to go out. A group of us usually went together. We swam, bowled, and went to movies and to restaurants. We also liked to congregate at a friends house to play cards, sing, listen to records, and just talk. Actually, we enjoyed doing the same things our sighted friends did.

It was at a New Year's Eve party that I met the only sighted man I ever dated regularly. He had come to the party with a former classmate of mine. We liked each other the moment we met. I'm sure I was flattered by his attention, for he was always attentive and thoughtful. It was nice to have a male escort who could take me wherever I wanted to go although a funny thing occurred the first time he brought me home from a date.

We went to the house next door. The minute we stepped onto the wooden porch I knew we were at the wrong place since the porch of the house where I lived was concrete. "This isn't where I live," I cried. Later I teased, "I don't believe you can see any better than I can."

Although we were never officially engaged, we did discuss marriage. Perhaps it is just as well we eventually broke up since we disagreed on some important issues. He wanted children; I didn't because my blindness is hereditary, and I didn't want to risk passing it on to future generations. He was a staunch Catholic; I was an even stauncher Baptist which could have caused problems. He was not as well educated as I.

After we had dated for awhile, I began to wonder why he didn't introduce me to his family. Whenever I expressed the desire to meet them, he would change the subject. Finally I demanded, "What's wrong? Don't you want me to meet your family?"

"You wouldn't like them," he answered. "Sometimes they aren't very nice."

"What do you mean?" I asked.

"I had hoped I wouldn't have to tell you how they feel about our dating," he said, "but I suppose you'll find it out sooner or later."

"You mean they object to it because I can't see," I cried.

"Please don't let it upset you," he begged. "How they feel about us doesn't matter. It's how we feel about each other that's important."

I should not have felt as angry, resentful, and hurt as I did. I knew their attitude was no different from that of many sighted individuals, but knowing something doesn't necessarily alleviate the pain and discomfort of feeling rejected.

It is odd how often we strike out at those we love, hurting them the way we are hurt when we become angry. "Well, I'd like to tell your family you're not such a prize," I exclaimed angrily. I hated myself for being so unkind, but I was too upset to retract my words.

"Do we have to continue talking about it?" he asked,

ignoring my remark. "Can't we forget it?"

"I can't," I stormed. "Maybe we shouldn't see each other for awhile. I need time to sort out my thoughts."

"All right," he acquiesced. "I'm sorry you are so upset. Call me when you've had time to think things through."

That night he went out of my life. I never called him although I wanted to. Once I picked up the phone and started dialing his number only to replace the receiver before I had finished. For weeks I was miserable. I had never before harbored such resentment. I knew I was not reacting as a Christian should. I began to pray for God's healing touch. Then sometime later my husband Park and I discovered each other.

Our first date was almost an accident. I heard about Park when he entered the school for the blind to complete his high school education after an accident in which he lost his sight. Before coming to school, he had spent several months in the hospital recuperating from the burns inflicted by the molten aluminum which had destroyed his sight and burned much of his body. However, it was not until I had finished college and returned to Louisville to work that we became acquainted when we went swimming.

That evening Park suggested I go swimming with him when neither the fellow who had asked me nor the girl he had invited showed up. Grateful for his invitation I readily accepted.

I really had fun that evening. Park was a good swimmer. He had brought along an inner tube which gave me more freedom since I couldn't swim. I was afraid conversing with him might be difficult, but I soon discovered we had several common interests. We both enjoyed good books, music, plays, and listening to some of the same radio programs. I decided I should like to know him better. Evidently he felt the same way about me since he

asked permission to come to see me. I agreed to see him if
he would promise not to become interested in me. I didn't
want to encourage him since I knew he was having
difficulty adjusting to his blindness. As for me, I had no
intention of becoming seriously involved with anyone
else, or so I thought.

I'm not sure when I began to fall in love with Park. I
remember it was not too long until I was listening eagerly
for my doorbell to ring the nights I was expecting him.

His first term of endearment for me was "honey child."
One of my birthday presents from him the first year we
dated was a cake with "Happy Birthday, Honey Child" on
it. Another of my gifts from him was a five-pound box of
Hershey kisses. Since he worked in a concession stand he
could buy candy wholesale. The next day at work I think I
shocked some of my friends when I informed them, "I'll
bet I got more kisses last night than any of you." Then I
proceeded to pass around the kisses he had given me.

The fall after we started dating, I invited Park to go
home with me one weekend to meet my parents. It was on
a Saturday night in our porch swing when he admitted
that, in spite of his good intentions not to, he had fallen in
love with me. I think he paid me one of the nicest
compliments I have ever received when he stated that my
attitude toward my handicap had done more than anything else to restore his self-confidence. He declared that
my optimism and enthusiasm were so contagious that
they had changed his outlook on life at a time when he
had felt that it was hardly worthwhile.

In November we became engaged. I recall how apolo-
getic Park was about not being able to give me a more
expensive ring. Several times during our marriage he has
suggested replacing it with a better one. I have always
refused since there are some things, including my inex-
pensive engagement ring, I consider priceless.

At the time we became engaged I was renting a furnished apartment in the home of some friends. As soon as we decided on the date of our wedding, we started looking for an unfurnished apartment. When we succeeded in finding one we began to buy, beg, or borrow enough furniture to furnish it. I moved into our apartment three weeks before our wedding.

Several days prior to our marriage I went home to discuss my wedding plans with my parents. I wanted the ceremony to be performed in the living room of my childhood home with my dad giving me away.

While I was there Mom and I had a long talk, the first one we had had for some time. During our conversation I asked her how she and Dad felt about my upcoming marriage since they still did not know Park too well.

"I suppose the parents of every blind child would like to see their child grow up to marry a person with perfect sight," she admitted. "However, your dad and I realize that things don't always work out that way."

"Does that mean you disapprove of my marriage to Park?" I demanded.

"Oh, no," she cried. "We think Park is a fine person. If you love him, you have our blessing."

I assured her that I expected to be happier with Park than I could ever be with anyone else.

"Then we are happy for you," she said squeezing my hand.

On February 22, 1942, Park and I were married at my childhood home. We had a quiet wedding with just my immediate family and a few very close friends present.

Perhaps it is true that only the characters in fairy tales live happily ever after. Nevertheless Park and I have had a good marriage. We both are glad and grateful that a loving God allowed our paths to cross.

5
Spills and Thrills
in the Kitchen

I, like many other visually impaired homemakers, have learned to laugh at my mishaps or "blind blunders" as we called them at school and to laughingly relate them to others. You are invited to laugh along with me as you read about some of my spills and thrills in the kitchen – and elsewhere.

Since I was a working wife from the time of my marriage in 1942 until my retirement in 1979, my husband has always assisted me with household chores. We both listed cooking as one of our hobbies. Park has won quite a reputation for himself as a good cook. Some of his specialities are soup, not out of a can, and cakes made from scratch. Two favorites are the butter cake and the tunnel of fudge cake.

Once after having given the recipes for these cakes to a sighted friend she called to lament, "I just made a tunnel of fudge cake, but when I attempted to remove it from the pan, my tunnel collapsed. What did I do wrong?"

I reminded her that the directions stated plainly, "Let cake cool in pan for two hours before removing it."

"Oh, dear!" she wailed. "I should have rechecked the recipe, but I thought I knew exactly what to do."

"Well, try again," I advised. "That's what I'd do. Only next time follow the directions."

By following the directions closely her next cakes were as delicious as Parks. She could hardly wait to tell us about the expressions of astonishment on the faces of friends at a church supper when she informed them she had obtained the recipe for her cake from a blind man.

I had not done much cooking when I, too, learned how important it is to follow instructions carefully. My husband still teases me about the first time I cooked rice. With no one around to read me the directions I decided to cook the entire box since I liked rice and since it can be used in a variety of ways. The grains seemed small as I filtered them through my fingers. As a result of my blunder, I had more than enough rice to last for several days even though I served it as a cereal, as a vegetable, with meat, in casseroles, in desserts, and every other conceivable way.

A question I am frequently asked by new acquaintances is, "Do you do your own cooking?"

"I'm afraid so," I reply with a chuckle, "since we can't afford a cook and since my husband has a healthy appetite."

Another question I am sometimes asked is, "How can you tell when your food is done?" If I know the person making the inquiry fairly well, I'm apt to respond, "Oh! I cook by smellevision." I then proceed to explain that the blind homemaker learns to rely on her remaining senses when preparing and cooking her food.

There is nothing more frustrating to the visually impaired cook than a recipe which simply states, "Cook until done," or "Bake until golden brown." I should like to say a word of commendation to the authors and editors of cookbooks who give specific instructions such as the exact timing and temperature.

In my opinion the *Better Homes and Gardens* cookbooks, several of which are available in braille, are excellent.

A number of other good cookbooks in braille and on

records or cassettes can be obtained. Several kitchen aids and appliances such as braille labels, timers, and thermometers have either been manufactured or adapted to meet the needs of the visually handicapped. These can be purchased from some agencies for the blind. Sometimes an appliance which meets a particular need can be found by browsing through the housewares of a local department store. Before making a purchase, one should make sure he can operate and take care of the merchandise successfully. Since all the blind are different, what works for one doesn't work for all of them.

Still other questions I have been asked are, "Do you ever open the wrong can?" or "Do you have difficulty distinguishing one product from another?"

Thanks to a good memory and my childhood training of having a specific place for things which I have carried over into my housekeeping, this happens less often than one might suspect. I have to admit, however, that occasionally I have been forced to change my menu at the last minute because I opened the wrong can or confused one product with another.

One of the worst errors I ever made was the time I fixed frozen squash for frozen apples. After emptying a bag of what I assumed to be apples into a baking dish and sprinkling them generously with brown sugar, cinnamon, and butter, I proceeded to bake them. I was not aware of my mistake until I removed them from the oven and tasted them. Since Park and I prefer squash as a vegetable and not a dessert, this concoction went down the garbage disposal.

One of my partial sighted friends tells a funny story about the time she opened a can of diced beets instead of red beans to go into her chili. She couldn't imagine what her husband was talking about, when he demanded

"What's in this chili," until she had tasted it for herself and discovered her error.

Once Park accidentally substituted the fresh orange juice I had stored in a milk carton in the refrigerator in the cream sauce he was preparing to go over chipped beef on toast. Needless to say I didn't file that recipe.

Not all "blind blunders" have such disastrous or perhaps I should say distasteful endings. One day I decided to make cherry delight, a dessert which requires a can of cherry pie filling. Since I was almost positive the only can of unlabeled pie filling on my pantry shelf was cherry, I opened it. I had previously removed the label to take advantage of a money back offer. Fortunately, my memory had served me well. The can I opened contained cherry pie filling.

A good rule for the visually handicapped cook to learn and apply is taste, smell, or touch all ingredients that go into a recipe before adding them.

All "blind blunders" do not occur in the kitchen. With the assistance of the store's personnel and a grocery list written in braille my husband does almost all our marketing. One day I wanted some Royal Anne cherries to go in a jello salad I had volunteered to supply for a bereavement dinner the Woman's Missionary Union of my church prepares for the family of a deceased member. I wrote Queen Anne instead of Royal Anne on the grocery list. Poor Park had the manager of the store and two or three employees vainly searching for the Queen Anne cherries.

Recently just outside a supermarket Park ran into someone or so he thought until he apologized, and something licked his hand. Upon investigating he discovered he had bumped into a big, woolly dog tied to a post.

One day while grocery shopping with a friend, I accidentally got hold of someone else's cart. Imagine my chagrin when a stranger responded to my inquiry, "Lorene, what is this?" "I'm not Lorene, and this isn't your cart."

Since I have always been an extremely busy person, I appreciate ready-prepared foods which are nutritious and appetizing. One we especially like is Stouffer's frozen corn souffle. More than one guest has requested my recipe when I served it.

Gladly I comply by telling them to go to the frozen food compartment of their nearest supermarket and pick up as many packages of Stouffer's corn souffle as needed. Then after paying for it at the checkout stand, take it home, and prepare according to directions on package.

It is gratifying to be able to share my recipes with both blind and sighted friends. Two of them, one for a cheese meat loaf, the other for a buttermilk pie, appeared in our church cookbook. Since so many have liked my buttermilk pie, I have included the recipe for it.

BUTTERMILK PIE

⅔ stick butter	1 tablespoon flour
3 eggs	1 teaspoon vanilla
1¼ cup granulated sugar	½ cup buttermilk
pinch of salt	1 9-inch unbaked pie shell

Melt butter over low heat and set aside to cool. In a bowl beat eggs, add sugar, salt, flour, vanilla, and buttermilk, blending well. Stir into melted butter. Pour into pie shell and bake at 350 degrees for 45 minutes.

This pie tastes very much like a chess pie. It keeps well in the refrigerator for two or three days if one is lucky enough to have some around that long.

Another dessert I enjoy baking is cookies. One Christmas I baked nine different kinds. That year I gave cookies as gifts to several friends. Some of them still expect a box of my homemade cookies under their Christmas tree. I consider this such a nice compliment that I try not to disappoint them.

Christmas is both a busy and a happy time at our house. One group I especially look forward to entertaining during the holidays is the Sunday School class I have been teaching the past thirty years. The largest number to attend one of my parties was the year Park donated us a twenty-pound turkey he had received as a gift from the owner of the building where he worked. Since he doesn't like turkey, he suggested I serve it at a covered-dish dinner for my Sunday School class. Thirty-three ladies showed up to share Park's turkey and all the trimmings which they helped provide.

My parties are not usually that elaborate although the women always seem to enjoy themselves. Frequently I make up the games we play at my Christmas parties and at the bridal and stork showers I have given over the years. Some of my Christmas games were published in the October-December, 1978, issue of *Church Recreation,* a Southern Baptist periodical. A Bible quiz I made up for a church gathering appeared in the April-June, 1980, issue of the same magazine.

Christmas is not the only time Park and I entertain visitors. We enjoy our friends who drop in throughout the year. Whenever we have dinner guests without sight, I seat them at the table and then serve their plates. It is easier for me to carry a filled plate from the stove to the table than to pass bowls of hot food. Fewer spills also occur. There is one drawback, however. Everyone may not get an equal portion of food, or he may not get some of everything on the menu. This has happened at least once at our house.

One evening after our guests had departed, my husband remarked, "Honey, I thought you were planning to have peas for dinner."

"I did have peas," I answered.

"Well, I didn't," he stated.

We have always wondered who got Park's peas.

Once when we were having dinner at the home of some blind friends, our hostess served a delicious broccoli casserole. Amid the compliments and questions regarding the ingredients and preparation of her casserole one of the guests exclaimed, "What casserole? I didn't get any."

On still another occasion our hostess, who was blind, inquired which of her guests wished coffee and which tea. I requested hot tea, my favorite beverage. After my first sip, I knew something was wrong with my drink. "What brand of tea is this?" I asked.

"Lipton, the same brand you use," she answered. "Why?"

"Well, I'm sorry, but it doesn't taste like Lipton tea to me," I declared.

"Oh, dear!" she cried. "I'll bet I put a tea bag in a cup in which there was instant coffee!"

"I'll bet you did, too," her husband stated. "You have given me a cup of plain hot water to drink."

I'll never forget how nervous I was the first time I invited Park's family for dinner. My day got off to a bad start when Park ran water in the tapioca pudding I had set in the sink to cool and forgotten to tell him it was there. Neither of us recall what we had for dessert that day, but we remember it was not tapioca pudding as originally planned.

One of the most successful parties I ever helped give was a reception at my home honoring my parents on their sixtieth wedding anniversary. Approximately one hundred friends and relatives came by to extend their good wishes to them.

I attempt to keep my home immaculate and attractive. Some of my nicest things are gifts from my husband. On Christmas, birthdays, and anniversaries, Park usually gives me something I want for the house but would not ordinarily buy for myself such as my crystal, my china, and a beautiful punch bowl.

I was really surprised the Christmas he gave me a chime clock. My sister Daisy was living next door at the time. On Christmas Eve we had gone to her house to exchange gifts. About five minutes before ten Park suggested we go home. He had timed it just right. The minute we walked in the door my clock began to chime the hour.

"Oh, you got me a chime clock!" I exclaimed throwing my arms around him.

"I may have messed up your decorations," he apologized. "I had to move some of them."

"It doesn't matter," I answered. I was so delighted with my clock I couldn't have cared less about Christmas decorations.

Although I am not a trained counselor, several individuals losing their sight have requested my help. I'm always glad for the opportunity to assist them. If possible I invite them to my home where we can talk in a relaxed atmosphere. The ladies are generally interested in any helpful household hints I can supply.

I distinctly remember how discouraged one couple was who called on us. The lady had already lost practically all her sight. I could sense her tension as I guided her to the couch. Her despair was obvious from the sound of her voice as she cited some of her frustrations. "Sometimes I don't know why I keep on trying, I do such dumb things," she lamented. "Why, last night I sprinkled nutmeg instead of black pepper on the chicken I was going to bake for dinner."

Although I laughed, I was quick to explain, "I'm not laughing at you but with you. Your experiences sound so much like what I call my 'blind blunders.' Let me tell you what happened to me today."

At a luncheon that day I had noticed the glass containing my cola felt fairly light when I picked it up. However, I thought nothing of it until I took a swallow of Sprite, the drink my neighbor had requested.

"You picked up your neighbor's drink," she exclaimed, laughing for the first time. "Weren't you embarrassed?"

"Of course," I answered, joining in her laughter. "I felt like crawling under the table."

During the evening I tried to point out to her in a roundabout way that self-pity is the worst possible handicap.

It was Park who suggested I tell her about the time I spilled the filling for a pie onto my clean kitchen floor. She seemed eager to hear. Sometimes hearing about another's imperfections helps to restore one's self-confidence.

Anyway, at the time, we were expecting dinner guests. I arose early to bake a cheese pie, a favorite dessert that usually turns out well. I mixed the filling for this pie in my electric blender. I was convinced the bottom of the container holding the pie filling was screwed on tightly, but apparently I was mistaken. When I picked it up, the contents spilled over the counter down the front of the cabinet and onto the kitchen floor instead of the empty pie shell.

I could have wept. Not only had I lost an hour's sleep but a luscious pie filling as well. Besides, there was the mess to clean up. That was one of the times I really had to count to twenty twice in order to remain calm, cool, and collected. However, at the count of thirty-nine I stopped ringing my hands, removed my shoes and stockings, picked up a wet soapy rag, got down on my knees and began to tidy up my kitchen.

The reason I remove my shoes and stockings when mopping the floor is that my bare feet are like an extra pair of hands in helping me locate whatever I spill. They also prevent me from tracking it onto the clean area should I step in it.

Moments later down on my knees wiping up the floor, I began to breathe a prayer of thanks for the vanilla ice cream stored in my freezer. After all, I was in the correct position for prayer.

When I say this, I am not being flippant. For, more than anything else, prayer has helped me cope with the ups and downs of life, including my spills and thrills in the kitchen.

Friends have brightened my life. In the spring of 1927 I posed with three of them (from left to right): Thelma Wood, Nancy Stacy, Dorothy Morrow, and guess who.

As a young adult I did proofreading with the Printing House for the Blind.

My husband, "Park," and I go for a stroll at our cozy home in Louisville *(Home Mission Board Photo by Jim Wright).*

What would I do without dear friends? Here I am dictating to Virginia Crawford *(HMB Photo by Wright).*

My sister, Daisy, and I talk about old times—and new. She is also blind *(HMB Photo by Wright).*

Technology is marvelous—practical. Here Park is using a talking calculator and I am holding a talking clock *(HMB Photo by Wright)*.

Technology again! I'm busy at my braille typewriter, a daily blessing *(HMB Photo by Wright)*.

With me in the middle, our family gathered to celebrate my parents' sixtieth wedding anniversary.

My pastor, Dr. Robert O. Williams, recently awarded me a certificate of appreciation on behalf of the church *(HMB Photo by Wright)*.

One of my "favorite things" is teaching the Word of God to my Sunday School class *(HMB Photo by Wright).*

Dr. Lucien Coleman, professor at Southern Seminary, is one of several professors who have encouraged my writing *(Photo by Rick Reynolds).*

6
The House That Jack Built

Exhausted, I fell into bed. Every muscle in my body ached. The house was still cluttered with boxes to be unpacked, and I didn't have the remotest idea which one contained our pajamas. Nevertheless, I had never felt happier. Another prayer had been answered; another dream come true; another goal attained. My husband and I were spending our first night in our new home.

As tired as I was, sleep was slow in coming. While I lay there awake, my thoughts drifted back almost ten years to the February night Park had carried me, his new bride, over the threshold of the apartment we had first called home.

Our apartment was in what had once been one of the loveliest old homes in the neighborhood. Shortly before our marriage, it had been sold, renovated, and converted into seven apartments. That night as I reminisced about past events, the same thought *How good God is* that always occurs to me each time I think back over my life flashed through my mind.

I recalled how fortunate Park and I had felt to find an apartment within walking distance of the American Printing House for the Blind, the place where I worked; Clifton Baptist Church, the church I attended; our doctor; our dentist; a variety of stores and shops, and two bus lines. Since I didn't travel alone, I hadn't wanted to move into a strange neighborhood.

I remembered the joys and some of the heartaches and frustrations that had come with the purchase of each new piece of furniture for our home. While Park and I have never quarreled violently, our worst arguments resulted from his reluctance to buy things on credit and my unwillingness to wait until we had sufficient cash to pay for our purchases.

We had not been married long when he began to save money for a phonograph. Each week he would put aside a portion of his earnings. Before he had accumulated the necessary amount, I found a floor lamp I wanted for our living room. I shall never forget how angry he became when I suggested we use some of the money he was saving to purchase it.

"Do you have to have that lamp immediately?" he demanded.

"No, but I want it," I answered.

"Helen, sometimes I don't understand you," he cried. "You're so reasonable about most things."

Grudgingly I agreed we could get the lamp later. I had to admit Park was correct in saying we would derive more pleasure from the phonograph since we both enjoy good music.

I am convinced the reason Park and I had such few arguments is that we have always discussed everything openly and candidly even though we sometimes disagree.

Occasionally we spend hours considering the pros and cons of a problem or project. For example, during World War II when the government was encouraging individuals to plant victory gardens, my husband wondered if he would not enjoy having one. He likes to watch things grow. Upon learning there was some ground available behind the building where we lived and that some of the tenants were planning to use it for gardens, he decided to request a plot. Although our neighbors seemed surprised, they gave him a space 16×90 feet that ran along the walk.

Everyone was amazed at his success. He set up stakes and strung heavy twine as guidelines between the rows and to separate his garden from the one adjoining it. Remembering how good the fresh food my mother had grown tasted, I encouraged him to plant a wide assortment of vegetables. He planted some of almost everything that grows well in this area.

Park really enjoyed gathering bags of fresh lettuce to take to our friends. That summer I did my first and only canning when he picked enough green beans for me to fill three quart jars. I don't know what I did wrong, but my beans spoiled. I was more successful with the vegetables I froze. The worst disappointment we experienced was the squirrels getting into our corn and destroying it when it was just about ready to boil on the cob. The weather the latter part of that summer was extremely hot and dry. Therefore, our late vegetables did not produce as much as we had hoped. Nevertheless, we were well pleased with the overall results of my husband's garden.

Another decision confronting us early in our marriage was whether or not we should rent a cheaper apartment which became available in our building. We finally concluded the five dollars a month we'd save would justify the move. However, we were mistaken. The third-floor apartment we moved into was not nearly as nice, nor as comfortable as the one we had previously occupied. It was too hot during the summer and too cold in the winter. I don't know how long we would have continued to live there if my sister Daisy and her husband had not become interested in investing in real estate. Since they were residing in the country at the time, they asked us to be on the lookout for a duplex they could purchase. We found two for sale on Bellaire. We felt one of them, a 12-room

frame house with a two-car garage, was a good invest-
ment. I was surprised when my husband suggested we
buy it after my sister and brother-in-law had decided to
purchase the other one.

"But honey, we've got only $1,100," I protested. "Do you
want to borrow $5,200?" That was the sum we would need
since the price of the house was $6,300. Suddenly, we had
exchanged roles. It was I who was objecting to our going
into debt.

"A house is different from other things. It's an invest-
ment," Park pointed out. "The downstairs will make an
ideal residence for us, and we can easily convert the
upstairs into two apartments."

He had no trouble convincing me since I wanted my
own home.

Negotiating a loan proved much more difficult than we
had anticipated. The first company we approached refused to consider our request. We assumed it was because
of our blindness. Naturally we resented this since we
were confident we could make the payments with the
money we collected from renting our apartments, plus
what we were paying in rent. The second company we
contacted agreed to lend us just about half the amount we
needed which was not nearly enough. Time was running
out, and we were becoming more and more discouraged
when someone suggested we apply for a loan from Avery
Savings and Loan. The people we talked to there were
much more understanding and a little more generous.
They agreed to lend us $4,300 which still would not have
been enough if we had not received help from some
unexpected sources. Three relatives and friends volunteered to lend us the remaining $900 we needed.

In September 1943, we moved again, this time to our
own home. We were soon familiar enough with our new
surroundings to get around with such ease and confi-

dence that Jess and Selma DeFever, a couple who came to look at one of our apartments were not aware of our handicap until after they had rented it. As they were leaving, Park informed them they could use the garage since we couldn't see and would not need it.

The DeFevers soon became some of our closest friends. Jess is now deceased, but we see Selma often. She still sews for me and helps me with my interior decorating.

Shortly after acquiring our home, we discovered another means of supplementing our income. We began to assemble and sell leather products such as wallets, coin purses, and link belts. Some of our friends started taking orders for us where they worked. For the next two years we had a thriving business. By using the income from this venture we were able to pay off our mortgage much sooner than we had expected.

Following his student days at the University of Louisville my husband was employed by the Kentucky Business Enterprises for the Blind, a government agency responsible for the training of visually impaired stand operators and securing concession stands for them in public buildings.

The information that the stand Park operated was to be abolished came as a shock to us. Job opportunities for the blind were much more limited then than now. I still recall the day I heard the news. The minute I inquired, "How was your day?" I knew something was wrong. At dinner Park ate little and spoke less. It was while we were doing the dishes that he said, "I hate to tell you this but the company where I work is closing my stand." Before I could comment he rushed on, "Thank goodness! They have consented to let me stay until I can find another job."

"Then we've nothing to worry about," I exclaimed in relief. "Your supervisor will find you another stand."

When days merged into weeks, and Park had not obtained another job, I began to worry. *What would he do if another stand did not become available? And how long would the company keep his stand open?* I wondered. Knowing how upset he was I tried to conceal my anxiety from him.

After several long weeks of waiting, we heard about a stand in a private firm Park might be able to get. If he could obtain it, it would be a perfect solution to our problem; for some time he had been wanting to go into business for himself. Immediately we contacted Mr. Huber, the president of the trucking terminal where the stand was located. He promised my husband the location if the heirs of the former owner were willing to sell him the equipment and stock. In the meantime someone else who was interested in obtaining the stand had approached them. However, after learning that Mr. Huber had promised Park the location, they reconsidered and accepted his offer.

Having his own business proved challenging and profitable. Park's income increased considerably since his new stand was much larger than the one he had worked in previously. Of course he had to spend more hours at work which meant he had less time to help me with household chores.

Now that we had some extra money available we decided to remodel our apartment. For some time, we had been wanting to make some alterations. We needed more storage space. There were no cabinets in our kitchen and only one small closet in our bedroom. I wanted an electric stove but couldn't have one since our house was not wired for 220-volt appliances. Our entire apartment needed redecorating.

We decided to begin our remodeling by having the paper steamed off our living room. It was soon evident that much of the plaster as well as the paper would have to be replaced. Since our paper hanger did not do plastering, we had to engage someone else for that which cost more than we had anticipated and took longer than we had expected. Furthermore, the house had never been so untidy. For days I could smell and taste dust from the plaster, and everything I touched felt gritty.

I was relieved when my husband observed, "I'm beginning to wonder if it would not be cheaper and less inconvenient to build a new house than to remodel an old one."

I thoroughly agreed with him. I had lost all desire to continue remodeling our apartment. The idea of building our own home appealed to me. If we could find a lot, we could have the kind of house we desired.

Once more we were extremely fortunate. My brother-in-law found a lot 50 × 300 feet we could buy just three blocks from where we lived. We contacted Earl Saunders, a friend we trusted, who was a contractor.

We spent hours discussing the house we wanted. Park drew a diagram of it in braille from which he and Earl could work out the details. The plans for our house included a fairly large living room and kitchen with built-in cabinets, a dining room, two bedrooms, plenty of closet space, a tile bath, and a full basement. Park left the interior decorating and the arranging of the furniture to our friend Selma and me. His only request being, "Please decide where you want things and leave them there." I knew why he made that request. When furniture is rearranged, it is frustrating to a person without sight.

It is thrilling to observe the construction of one's future home. Since we lived nearby, we could keep a constant lookout on the progress being made.

On a cold, bleak December day our house was completed except for the landscaping which Earl postponed until spring. We moved into it December 20, 1951. The only decorating I did that year was to hang a wreath on the front door and to put a Christmas tablecloth on my dining room table.

Our first guest was a friend of my husband's who worked at Huber's. When he called to ask if he and his wife could come by, he commented, "I want to see the house that Jack built." Everyone where Park worked called him Jack.

From then on I referred to our new home as the house that Jack built.

Shortly after we moved in, two groups, my Sunday School class and some of our friends, surprised us with house warmings. As we were opening our gifts at one of the parties the lady helping me started laughing. "What's so funny?" I demanded.

"Things are not always what they seem," she replied still chuckling. "From what is written on this box I thought you were receiving an 18-hour bra, but it's some guest towels that just match your bathroom." The gift was from a blind friend completely unaware of the writing on the box she had used.

At the same time we were planning our house, Park ordered fruit trees and grapevines to plant on the back of our lot. Except for the pear and apple trees they were a disappointment. The neighborhood kids, squirrels, birds, and insects reaped more benefit from them than we. For several years we had hard pears which were not too good to eat raw but were excellent for canning and preserving to share with our friends. We also harvested enough apples to freeze and to make applesauce.

One day my attention was attracted by the rattling of pots and pans. "What are you doing?" I asked Park.

"I'm going to make some applesauce," he responded.

"The apples are so faulty, I wouldn't bother," I remarked.

"You don't have to bother," he answered. A little later he called, "Come and taste my applesauce."

"It's delicious," I declared after tasting it. "Go get another bucket of apples. Let's make some more."

One spring day while Park and I were outside, someone hailed us just as a plane passed overhead. Not hearing his voice too well I assumed it was an out-of-town cousin whom we were expecting. Rushing up to him, I threw my arms around him and gave him a regular bear hug. When he spoke again, I realized I had made a mistake. The person I had hugged was our contractor who had come by to talk about our landscaping. I didn't help the situation any when I apologized, "I'm sorry, but I thought you were someone else."

We had not been living in our new home long when I began to lose my appetite and my energy and to feel tired most of the time. The doctor discovered I had low blood pressure and was anemic. He suggested I take a leave of absence when I failed to respond to the medicine he had prescribed for me. Instead of requesting a leave of absence I decided to ask my supervisor to let me work part-time since I liked being busy and really needed to work. I had bought several things for our new home. She consented to let me work at home until I felt better.

Once I had adjusted to the change, Park and I liked the arrangement so well that I continued to work at home until my retirement in 1979.

My husband worked in his stand until 1965 when another trucking firm bought the company and moved to a new location in the county.

After much deliberation, Park decided, instead of looking for another stand, to turn our basement into a workshop and to start caning some chairs. Two unusual cane pieces I prize highly are a wastepaper basket which he designed especially for me and a footstool made from the spindles that held up the banisters in the old school building for the blind. At the time the building was razed Park and a friend were making footstools. When I wanted a memento of the old school, Park conceived the idea of making one out of the spindles he persuaded the superintendent to give him.

We still live in the house I jokingly refer to as the house Jack built. However, we are both aware that we owe not only our house but whatever success we have attained to the Master Builder. For "Except the Lord build the house, they labour in vain that build it" (Ps. 127:1).

7
How Do You Do?

Early in life I became accustomed to answering questions pertaining to my blindness. For example, one day when my chum and I stopped by a country store a bystander accosted me with, "How long have you b-b-been blind?"

"All my life," I answered.

"And nothing can be d-d-done for your eyes?" he wanted to know.

"No, sir," I informed him. "As yet, no remedy has been found for my blindness."

"Are you t-t-totally blind?" was his next question.

"Yes, I am," I responded.

Whereupon he began to pat his foot vigorously and to chant, "Oh! what a pit-pit-pity. You're such a l-l-lovely child. What a pit-pit-pity."

As we left the store, I was feeling as sorry for him with his speech impediment as he did for me although I was not as vocal about it.

The questions regarding blindness that follow are designed to help sighted individuals relate to the visually handicapped and to erase all traces of pity for them. The answers are based on my personal experiences, observations, and convictions.

Q: *Do you consider blindness a handicap?*

A: Yes, only an idealist would say the lack of sight is not a handicap. However, no one is perfect. Everyone has limitations or handicaps, and many people society has classified as handicapped have attained success by developing their remaining senses, using their ingenuity, and taking advantage of their opportunities.

Q: *Do you feel the blind are discriminated against?*

A: At times, yes. But almost everyone is discriminated against at one time or another. Since I am basically a happy person who prefers to think positively, I play down the negatives, concentrating on the pluses not life. Of course, as a Christian, I should like to see less discrimination.

Q: *What are some of the fears that sometimes prevent the visually impaired from joining sighted groups and participating in their activities?*

A: One of the greatest fears is that of not being accepted as one is. No normal person considers it a compliment to be regarded as a genius for doing simple, everyday tasks. He is equally upset when thoughtlessly treated as if he were not too bright.

Another fear results from one's inability to move around freely in strange surroundings. One is afraid of making an unfavorable impression or arousing the pity of one's sighted peers. The majority of the blind appreciate the sympathy and understanding of others but resent their pity.

Still another source of worry is the attitude of some sighted individuals who hold themselves aloof refusing to get involved. Those individuals have either never known a handicapped person intimately or are afraid the handicapped will make too many demands on them.

Q: *Does a blind person in a sighted group feel a part of the group or more like an outsider?*

A: It depends on the person. One who is neat, outgoing, willing to get involved, and not overly sensitive about his or her handicap should soon experience a sense of belonging. I have never felt like an outsider of any group I have joined.

Q: *When conversing with the visually handicapped, should one avoid the use of words associated with blindness such as "blind," "see," and so forth?*

A: Absolutely not. Failure to use certain words doesn't alter a situation. It only limits one's vocabulary. However, since I am an individual with a name, I prefer a member of my Sunday School class saying, "Helen Parker, my Sunday School teacher," instead of "That blind lady who teaches my Sunday School class."

Q: *Should a sighted individual volunteer to help a blind person or should he wait until his assistance is requested?*

A: If you truly enjoy helping others, by all means volunteer your services. I am deeply grateful to those who volunteer their help whether or not I accept it. Don't become upset should your offer of help be refused. The person may not need it, or he may prefer to ask someone else for aid. Don't feel guilty if you cannot give the help requested. The average person will accept a reasonable explanation. He, too, is sometimes forced to change his plans. However, if your offer is a hollow gesture, don't make it. It is frustrating to be refused time after time. If you cannot give the help requested, don't solicit the services of another without first consulting the one desiring the help. He may prefer to ask someone else.

Q: *How much help should a volunteer be expected to give?*

A: Tell the person you plan to assist how much time you can spend. Find out in advance what help is needed. Don't allow the person to make unnecessary demands on you.

Q: *What suggestions do you make to help the visually handicapped relate to the sighted?*

A: If the visually handicapped wish to be accepted by the sighted, they must try to make the best possible impression. Always be courteous whether accepting or declining help. Practice saying please and thank you, words that will endear you to others. Don't get too upset when someone does or fails to do something that offends you. Chances are it was not deliberate. I have discovered that the majority of people are basically kind, but many of them know little or nothing about the blind. You may be the first blind person they have encountered.

Discourage well-meaning individuals from thinking you are unusual because you teach a Sunday School class, have a bowling score slightly above average, or can bake a cake. Remember your next cake may fall or burn.

Q: *What advice do you give sighted parents of a visually handicapped child?*

A: The knowledge that your child is handicapped usually produces shock, a guilt complex, resentment, or depression. The sooner you learn to conceal your feelings and start to accept your child the way he is, the quicker both you and he will adjust to his handicap. Every child is entitled to a good self-image. Your feelings about his condition will determine the kind of self-image he acquires.

Try not to spoil your child. Encourage him to be as independent and self-reliant as possible.

Q: *How can other family members help the one who loses his sight later in life?*

A: Resume normal family relationships at the earliest possible moment. Try to conceal your feelings of anxiety from him. If you or he has trouble adjusting, consult your minister or a professional Christian counselor. Learn what services are provided for the blind.

Q: *How does one go about obtaining this information?*

A: Contact your nearest state office of vocational rehabilitation. They will inform you what services are available and refer your case to the proper resource people.

Q: *Is it better to be born blind or to lose one's sight later in life?*

A: Opinions differ on the subject. Those born blind usually accept and adjust to their handicap easier than those who have once seen. On the other hand those who have seen can visualize their surroundings and can perform some tasks better than those blind from birth.

Q: *Is it easier to travel with a cane or a guide dog?*

A: Again opinions differ. If you like animals and are willing to assume the responsibility of caring for a guide dog, you will probably want to use a dog. If you dislike animals, by all means learn to use a cane unless, like me, you prefer to rely on friends or a taxi to take you where you need to go.

Q: *Do you visualize your surroundings including your friends?*

A: I have a mental picture of my surroundings including the people I encounter, but I'm sure it differs from the one a sighted person has. For example, when I picture a person, I think of personality traits and the sound of his voice rather than his physical features.

Q: *Does color mean anything to the blind?*

A: It depends on whether the person is born blind or loses his sight later in life. Color means little to one who is blind from birth. However, in order to be better informed I have learned as much as possible about it. For example, by questioning others I know what colors look best on me. Should I attempt to describe something involving color, I would have to verbalize. A person having seen colors maintains a mental image of them. My husband who could see until he was sixteen still dreams in color. I do not.

Q: *How do you shop for your clothes?*

A: I request the help of a sighted friend whose opinion I value. Occasionally, if I know exactly what I want, I telephone a store and have the merchandise delivered to my home. Some individuals rely on the salesperson for help. I do not.

Q: *How do you coordinate your clothes?*

A: When I make a purchase, my first question is, "What color is it?" I then inquire, "What color accessories should I wear with it?" Often I hang tops and slacks or blouses and skirts that go together on the same hanger.

Q: *Would you buy merchandise your friend disliked if you liked it?*

A: No, since I chose someone to shop with me whose judgment I trust, I would not. However, I would not buy something she liked if I disliked it.

Q: *How do you apply your makeup?*

A: I use cake powder in order not to spill powder on my clothes. I use cream rouge which I apply with my fingertips. I apply my lipstick by rubbing the tube between my lips then pressing them together. Since I have never used eye makeup, I have no suggestions to offer about applying it.

Q: *How do you shop for groceries?*

A: With his white cane, a grocery cart, a braille list, and the assistance of one of the store's employees my husband does almost all our grocery shopping at a nearby supermarket. Since he is familiar with the store, he prepares his list so the person helping him will not have to backtrack. He chooses a time to shop when the store is less crowded and the personnel are not so busy.

Q: *How does a blind couple separate their groceries after purchasing them?*

A: I rely on sighted friends to help me separate the things I cannot identify by touch. I then put them in a specific place I have designated for them. Some of my blind friends label their groceries in braille.

Q: *How do you avoid accidents in the kitchen such as burning or cutting yourself?*

A: I avoid accidents by concentrating on what I am doing. I place knives with their cutting edge down. A blind homemaker avoids burns like a burned child dreads fire. I use long oven mitts to remove food from the oven. I turn pot handles away from me.

Q: *How do you measure the ingredients that go into your recipes?*

A: I use a set of measuring cups and a set of measuring spoons. These can be purchased at a department store.

Q: *How do you find things you drop?*

A: If I drop something on a hard surface, I can sometimes locate it by hearing where it fell. If I did not hear it fall, I have to feel for it. Frequently I use a yardstick, raking it across the floor until it strikes the object I am looking for. Occasionally, I get disgusted and wait until I step on it, or until someone comes in with sight who will find it for me.

Q: *How do you do your banking?*

A: Since there is a branch bank near our home, my husband, with the help of a bank employee, takes care of our banking. He can sign and endorse our checks. We keep a braille record of our deposits, withdrawals, and interest.

Q: *Is there any way you can identify bills?*

A: If there is, I have not discovered it.

Q: *How do you keep up with your money?*

A: After getting my bills identified, I fold them in a certain way. I can recognize currency by touch.

Q: *If a blind person gives you the wrong change in a business transaction, should you tell him about it?*

A: By all means. If he is honest, he will want to correct his error. If dishonest, he deserves exposure. What he does not appreciate is your discussing his mistake with others instead of him. The same thing applies to a blind workman who does a job for you.

Q: *How does a blind couple get their mail read?*

A: They have to rely on a sighted volunteer. Should a blind person request you to read his mail, don't discuss it with others. Don't read it to yourself then paraphrase it or interpret it for him. Read exactly what is there.

Q: *What can churches do to integrate the visually handicapped?*

A: If your church has several members, you may want to do some of the things my church, the Clifton Baptist Church, in Louisville, Kentucky, is doing. A committee consisting of both blind and sighted members try to discover the needs of the visually impaired and to suggest ways the church can meet those needs. The following needs have been met: Transportation to and from church is provided. Cassette tapes of the church paper are made and distributed to members who cannot read the print edition. Monthly shopping trips to outlying shopping centers are scheduled. A sighted guide accompanies each blind shopper, assisting him to get from store to store and to make purchases. A children's day out for the students of the Kentucky School for the Blind who attend our church is planned periodically. A family invites a blind child to sit with them during the morning worship service and go home with them to spend the day. Whenever possible, individual needs are met such as providing transportation to and from a doctor's office. Clifton cooperates with the civic groups in sponsoring projects that benefit the blind. It utilizes the talents of its handicapped members whenever possible. In 1980, Clifton sponsored the first retreat for the blind to be held in Kentucky at Cedarmore, our state Baptist camp.

Q: *What are some of the jobs the visually handicapped can do at church?*

A: Those qualified can teach Sunday School, hold class offices, work in WMU (a missions organization for women), play the piano, sing in the choir, serve on committees, and plan programs. However, not all the visually impaired are qualified to hold positions of leadership.

Q: *What do you do at your church?*

A: I teach Sunday School, am mission support and mission study chairperson for the WMU, serve on the committee for the visually handicapped, am program chairperson for a bimonthly prayer breakfast, and represent my church on a woman's committee that works with the Southern Baptist Theological Seminary to provide scholarships.

Q: *What are some of the ways individual members can help the visually handicapped?*

A: Offer them transportation to and from church and to church-related activities such as class meetings. Should they need assistance in getting around the church, offer to help them. Speak to them, calling them by name and identifying yourself. At church suppers either volunteer to walk through the line with them or to bring them their food, whichever they prefer. At a party, if something funny happens, tell them why everyone's laughing. Describe any visual aids being used. To summarize, just practice all the courtesies you would appreciate receiving if you were in their position.

Q: *What is the best method of enlisting a visually handicapped prospect?*

A: Visitation is by far the best method of enlisting a prospect, blind or seeing. Encourage him to talk about himself. The more he talks, the more information you can obtain and the easier it will be for you to relate to him. If you are ill at ease in his presence try to conceal it. Phrase your questions and remarks in such a way that you appear interested rather than curious. Don't be overly morbid or overly cheerful.

Q: *Can you recommend a standard approach?*

A: Not really, since no two people are alike. Try to identify with the particular person you are helping. Don't expect a newly blind person to be as well adjusted as one blind from birth. Remember the newly blind have to adjust to a whole new way of life. They are likely to be more self-conscious about their blindness.

Q: *What suggestions can you make to sighted Sunday School teachers who teach the visually handicapped?*

A: When teaching adults, introduce them to all class members including visitors. Describe slides, pictures, or other visual aids you use. Explain the information you write on the board. Encourage them to participate in class discussions and to attend class meetings. Tell them about the resources available to the blind if they are not aware of them. Make sure they are never left stranded.

When teaching children, remember the visually handicapped child can clap his hands as gleefully, shout as lustily, ask as many questions, get into as much mischief, and do as many constructive things as his sighted classmates if given the proper incentive. Provide that incentive. Should you feel inadequate to work with the exceptional child, conceal your feelings. In time they will disappear. Win the confidence of the child and that of his guardian. The first Sunday he attends Sunday School show him the room, allowing him to touch the various objects. Should a sighted child comment on his blindness, do not reprimand him or attempt to silence him. Instead explain simply and frankly that the new pupil cannot see. You might say, "Since Jack can't see, I'm showing him our room." Treat his blindness as if it were an ordinary event. Your pupils will likely follow your example in their acceptance of him.

Some additional help may be required for the blind child to participate in certain activities. Provide this assistance. Sometimes a sighted pupil can render this service. This is advantageous since it teaches the sighted child to be kind and considerate of a less fortunate classmate. It enhances the friendship of the two children as they work together as a team, and it gives the teacher more time for other duties. There will be a few activities the blind child cannot engage in successfully. Yet if she is not kept busy she will become bored and her interest in Sunday School will wane. Substitute an activity she can engage in. For example, she could work with modeling clay while the sighted children draw.

The following don'ts should prove helpful:

When in doubt, don't be afraid to experiment. Don't allow the handicapped child to monopolize your time. Explain to him there are other pupils who also need your attention. Don't allow him to manipulate you or his classmates by persuading you to do things for him he is competent to do for himself. Don't expect all visually handicapped pupils to be alike. Never forget the handicapped child is probably in Sunday School because he and his parents regard you as an understanding friend and wise teacher. Don't let them down.

Q: *What resources are available for those with impaired vision who attend church-related activities?*

A: The Sunday School Board of the Southern Baptist Convention publishes two monthly magazines in braille, the *Braille Baptist* and *Youth Braille Baptist*. In October the Board began publishing a taped edition of the Sunday School lessons. This material can be ordered through your church. Another periodical containing the Sunday

School lessons, Uniform Series, is the *John Milton Sunday School Quarterly*. Both braille and talking book editions are available free upon request. Contact your regional library for the blind for a complete list of Christian periodicals available. Your library can also supply you with a number of religious books in braille or on talking books. A braille or talking book edition of the Bible and braille concordance can be purchased from the American Bible Society. Several cassette books can be purchased from Christian book stores.

Q: *What characteristics do you possess that have helped you attain success as a church leader and Christian writer?*

A: A deep, abiding faith in God, a keen sense of humor, my love for people, and an intense desire to succeed. I believe two of these characteristics, my faith in God and my sense of humor, also make me the optimistic person I am.

Q: *Are your attitudes typical of the blind?*

A: Not necessarily. Not all blind people have the same attitudes. However, I am confident that many of them feel as I do.

Q: *Do you believe it is possible for a blind person to live a happy, productive life?*

A: Yes, a thousand times yes. If I did not, I should not have written this book. Hopefully my story is proof positive that a totally blind person can live a happy, productive life.

Q: *Is it better for a visually impaired person to marry a sighted spouse or someone similarly handicapped?*

A: At sometime in life every blind person has probably dreamed of marrying someone with perfect sight. But since love is blind, things don't always work out according to our dreams. Personally I think the choice of one's spouse should be based on the kind of individual he or she is rather than on the degree of his or her vision. Marry someone whose ideals and values are similar to yours regardless of whether or not the person can see.

I have been asked these questions about my writing:

Q: *How do you write?*

A: I use a braille writer. Unlike a typewriter it only has six keys, one for each of the six dots that constitute a braille unit. The keys for dots 1, 2, and 3 are to the left of the space bar. Those for dots 4, 5, and 6 to the right. Since *a* is dot 1, I press that key to write *a*. Should I wish to write *b,* I press the keys for dots 1 and 2. Because it is harder for me than for a sighted writer to make corrections, I do as much composing as possible in my mind before I sit down to write. Once I have decided what I wish to convey I write the first draft of my manuscript. I continue going over it, making revisions or rewriting until it is as good as I can make it. I then dictate it to a sighted typist who takes it down in shorthand and types it for me. I can type, but since so much of my work has to be done according to specifications, and since I cannot correct my errors or proofread it, I prefer to employ a sighted typist.

Q: *How do you do research?*

A: Research is one area in which I truly feel handicapped. I have a braille concordance which I use to locate Scripture passages in my braille Bible. I use my cassette player for taping interviews. I can obtain some material I need in braille or on records from my regional library. I have to rely on sighted help for any other research I do.

Q: *Where do you get the ideas for your writing?*

A: My ideas come from my experiences, observations, convictions, imagination, and books. I keep my mind open and my ears attuned for anything that will provide me subject matter for an article, story, or devotional.

Q: *What is your favorite form of writing?*

A: I prefer to write devotional material, although I find it challenging to do other types of writing.

Q: *How do you handle your rejections?*

A: I wish I could say, "I do not get any rejections." However, since I cannot, I quip, "My acceptances keep me writing; my rejections keep me humble."

Q: *How long do you plan to continue writing?*

A: Until I can no longer think clearly since I regard my writing as a means of witnessing.

Q: *What advice would you give beginning writers?*

A: If at first you don't succeed, write, write, and keep writing.

Q: *Are you offended when someone thoughtlessly asks you a question you can't answer because of your blindness? For example, who is that dark-haired lady over there with the green dress on.*

A: No. Actually, I feel flattered that he has momentarily forgotten I cannot see. I consider it an indication that he regards me as not too different from his other acquaintances.

Q: *Do you object to being asked questions about yourself or your blindness?*

A: No, since I appreciate their curiosity. I like to learn as much as possible about the people I encounter. It is easier for me to relate to someone I know fairly well than to an individual I know nothing or little about.

Q: *What is the strangest question regarding your blindness you were ever asked?*

A: Undoubtedly the strangest question I was ever asked regarding my blindness was, "What are the advantages of blindness?" For a moment I wondered if my ears had deceived me. I'm sure my voice rose slightly when I demanded, "What did you say?"

"What are the advantages of blindness?" he repeated.

"I'm sorry, sir," I exclaimed still aghast, "but there are

no advantages. I can't think of a single one."

"But there must be some," he insisted. "I should think not seeing the frowns and scowls on people's faces would be an advantage."

"Oh, but I can recognize a disgruntled person by the tone of his voice," I cried. As I spoke, I recalled some occasions when I had perceived and appreciated some things my seeing friends had missed or had taken for granted.

"Well," I conceded, "perhaps there might be an advantage or two."

I promptly put his very strange question out of my mind, confident he had intended no offense. Actually, I didn't think of it again until one night while reading a novel in braille long after my husband was asleep. Suddenly I thought, *How fortunate I am to be able to read as well at night as during the day. Would an avid sighted reader consider this an advantage of blindness?*

For the next few days I deliberately searched for other advantages. As strange as it may seem, these are the ones I discovered. Many a teenager coming home late at night and trying to crawl into bed undetected might envy the ease with which a blind person can move quietly through his house any hour of the day or night.

Laughingly, my husband and I tell our friends that one of the ways we are fighting inflation and conserving energy is by not turning on lights. With utility bills skyrocketing the way they are, some of them may consider this an advantage.

Another advantage is the new friends I have acquired when an unselfish person has gone out of his way to help me because of my blindness.

My handicap has also opened some doors which have enabled me to share my faith through the written and spoken word.

These discoveries have convinced me that a handicap like retirement can become a stepping-stone instead of a stumbling block by those who take advantage of their advantages. Now that I have joined the ranks of senior citizens, my supreme desire is to use both my handicap and my retirement to replace the furrows, frowns, and scowls on the faces of some of God's unhappy, misguided children with smiles of joy and victory, even though I cannot see them.

8
Lend an Eye

The day I graduated from Centre College was truly a red-letter day in my life. I vividly recall the exact words of the president of Centre when he awarded me my degree. He called my name, "Helen Wallace," then that of my reader, "Lucy Anna Brooks." As we crossed the platform together, he remarked, "Two degrees won on one pair of eyes."

His comment was followed by thundering applause. I was the first blind graduate of Centre.

I've had occasion to ponder his statement many times since the day I graduated, for I am aware how much I owe Lucy Anna and countless others who were willing to lend an eye to me and my fellow blind. Our lives have been greatly enriched by the love and help they have so freely given.

My immediate family were the first people to lend me an eye. Every visually handicapped person needs a kid brother like the one I had. He began leading my sister and me almost as soon as he could walk by himself. He'd come up to us, take our hands, and exclaim, "I lead you, I lead you."

While he was still quite small, I discovered I could bribe him and some of his little friends to do almost anything I wanted done by telling them a story. They enjoyed the ones I made up as much as those I had read or heard. Sometimes I read them stories about a goose from a book, *Dr. Gander,* I had won as a prize at school. That gave me an idea. I began making up stories to tell them about a blind girl who owned a talking guide dog. Of course my fictitious dog was much more intelligent, imaginative, and adventurous than a regularly trained animal. He was constantly getting his mistress in trouble. However, he loved her too dearly to allow her to get hurt and often risked his life to save her from some peril.

Once when my brother observed some kids pretending to be blind, he misinterpreted their play as ridicule. A fight would have ensued had I not intervened, explaining to him they were only playing.

Mom taught him and my sighted sister how important it was not to move Daisy's and my possessions without our consent and knowledge.

Another way in which my mother helped me was by describing each new piece of my wearing apparel. As I ran my fingers over it, she would tell me its color and the colors that would go well with it. In this way I learned to coordinate my clothes. I still follow this procedure whenever I make a purchase. Although I refer to my clothes by their color, I distinguish one garment from another by the texture of the material or the way it is made. For example, when I was a little girl two of my favorite dresses were a pink voile and a blue print. I recognized my pink dress by its tucked bodice and the blue one by its buttons.

One Sunday Mom suggested I wear my print dress to church. When I was ready to go, she observed, "You've got on your pink dress. I thought you were going to wear your blue print."

"I couldn't," I replied, "one of the buttons was missing." With my sensitive fingers I had discovered the missing button my mother had overlooked when she laundered it.

My parents were not overly protective of me. They

encouraged me to make sighted friends and to participate in as many of their activities as possible. Whenever I wished, I could invite my playmates to our house to play.

My parents took me to Sunday School, enrolling me in the class in which I belonged. It was there that I met Lucy Anna when we were both ten and almost all of my other sighted playmates. I soon started going to and from my Sunday School class with one of them and sitting with them during the worship service. One or more of them would usually go home with me on Sunday or I'd spend the day with them. I visited some of them often enough to learn my way around their houses quite well.

Since I attended a rural church, resource material was not as widely used there as in a larger church. However, the majority of my teachers made sure I understood any visual aids they used. One activity I excelled in was memorizing Bible verses.

Although I had always gotten along well with the sighted kids in my neighborhood, I had a few misgivings when it was time to enter college. *Could I compete with sighted students? And would they accept me socially?* I wondered. My misgivings were short-lived. I had no trouble keeping up with my classes, and I soon had several good friends. Only one professor tried to discourage me from taking his course. He explained that he assigned so much supplementary reading he was afraid I might not be able to keep up. Since I am not easily daunted, and since I really wanted to take that course, I refused to be dissuaded. I shall never forget his astonishment when I made the highest grade of anyone in the class on his first test. What a nice way to say, "I told you so."

Shortly after my enrollment at college a reporter on the school paper requested permission to write a feature story about me. At first I was reluctant to consent. I have always discouraged well-meaning individuals from thinking me unusual for doing the things I consider normal. In my opinion, as yet, I had done nothing at Centre to merit acclaim. While Kathleen, the reporter, understood my position, she reminded me I was the first blind person to attend Centre. Furthermore, I was probably the only person without sight the majority of the faculty and student body had ever known. Naturally they were interested in learning more about the visually handicapped. She promised not to write anything that did not meet with my approval. She finally convinced me that my story would be interesting, informative, and beneficial to my relationships with fellow students.

Once I had consented, I cooperated with her fully. Together we decided her article would not only tell some of my hobbies and aspirations but would list some do's and don'ts for helping the blind. I even suggested some facts pertinent to blindness for her to include.

Her article was well received. Some students who heretofore had remained aloof or had seemed ill at ease at my presence became friendly and helpful once they realized how much I had in common with them despite my blindness. Like almost all of them I was attending college to prepare for a career. Like them I was anticipating marriage, having my own home, and finding my niche in life. Meanwhile, I enjoyed dating, parties, movies, and so forth as much as they.

Since becoming a free-lance writer, I have written similar articles to Kathleen's which have appeared in periodicals of various age groups for the Sunday School Board of the Southern Baptist Convention. A summary of the material I have included follows:

Many sighted individuals have the misconception that all of the visually handicapped are somewhat alike. For example, a new acquaintance once said to me, "I suppose you play the piano." When I had to admit that I didn't, she seemed disappointed simply because she had previously known a blind musician. I pointed out to her that not all the visually impaired are Tommy Sullivans or Helen Kellers, just as not all the sighted are Albert Einsteins or Archie Bunkers.

A lack of sight is the only thing many of the blind have in common. Among them you will meet saints and sinners, the brilliant and the mentally retarded, those well adjusted to their handicap and those who will probably never adjust to it. Their attitudes and aspirations are not the same. They appreciate being thought of and treated as individuals instead of being stereotyped. Judge them as you would others on whether or not they can do a job and how well.

Remember not all the blind need the same kind and amount of help. Should they refuse your assistance, respect their wish to be as independent as possible and continue to offer your help anytime it is appropriate. If in doubt regarding the aid they need, don't hesitate to question them about it. The majority will gladly supply you the information you desire.

Do not treat a person without sight as if he were deaf by speaking in an abnormally loud voice or by discussing him with others referring to him as he or as if he were not present.

I shall never forget a conversation my husband and I overheard between two ladies seated directly behind us on a bus. One of them commented, "They just wear watches to be like other people; of course, they can't tell time." Before her companion could answer, Park inquired, "Helen, what time is it?" Whereupon I opened my watch, felt the raised dots and announced the correct time. We never heard another word from either of them.

When addressing a blind person, speak to him directly,

calling him by name, or touch him gently. Never grab his cane. If it is necessary to terminate a conversation, excuse yourself. Don't just walk away leaving him talking to the wind. Do not embarrass him by changing your voice or inquiring, "Who am I?" Identify yourself if he does not know you well. In a group it is thoughtful to include him in the conversation by directing a remark to him or by asking a question. Call his name so he will know he is being addressed.

Never pet a guide dog without first getting permission from its master.

When calling on a visually handicapped person, replace any of his possessions you move. When helping him locate an object, give specific directions such as "To your right." Don't say, "Over there," meaningless words to the blind. Remember to turn off lights and to close cabinet doors and drawers. Do not leave a glass on the edge of a table or counter where he is likely to knock it off. When serving him food tell him when you are placing it before him so he will not accidentally put his hand in it or upset his beverage. Don't continue to put food on his plate or to refill his cup without inquiring if he wishes it.

If you are escorting a person without sight, allow him to hold onto your arm. When traveling by car, place his hand on the handle of the car door.

At a restaurant guide him to a table placing his hand on the back of a chair. Read him the menu including prices. If it is his turn to treat or he has invited you out, allow him to pick up the check. See that he gets whatever help he needs with his food. In a cafeteria tell him what is available, so he can choose the food he desires. It is thoughtful to mention the things that look especially appetizing.

In a store when helping a blind shopper, give him an honest appraisal of the merchandise. Tell him if the color and style are not becoming. However, leave the final decision as to whether or not he wishes to make the purchase up to him. When helping a person without sight shop for groceries, tell him if the produce or meat does not look fresh. If you cannot find the brand he wants, don't substitute another without his consent. Do not leave him standing alone in a public place without informing him of your intention.

On a trip it is thoughtful to describe things of interest to a sightless individual. Because he can't see something doesn't mean a lack of interest in it. My husband and I have taken numerous short trips and have gone on several delightful vacations with sighted friends. We try to select good guides as well as congenial companions.

Some places of interest we have visited are Niagara Falls; Williamsburg, Virginia; Greenfield Village; Warm Springs, Georgia; Cherokee, North Carolina; and the Smoky Mountains. We have toured several state parks in Kentucky and Indiana. For the past four or five years we have gone to the mountains of Kentucky with a good friend, Rosa Rodgers, to visit her family. On our first trip there we went to the Oneida Baptist Institute, a Southern Baptist boarding school where we had the pleasure of meeting and talking with Barkley Moore, the school's dedicated president.

Our favorite vacation spot is Florida. I shall always remember my first trip to the beach. As I stood at the water's edge, tasting its saltiness, feeling its spray on my face, and hearing the lapping of the waves on the shore, I could readily understand why and how nature has always evoked man's praise of God. Visiting an orange grove and picking my first orange was another thrilling experience. I enjoyed touching and tasting other tropical plants. Park and I like to go on guided tours since the guides are able to point out things of interest we might otherwise miss.

We especially enjoyed our tours of Saint Augustine and Cape Canaveral.

Our first airplane trip was to Florida. Since then, we have flown several times. The hostesses and other airline employees have always been courteous, pleasant, and helpful. For a while I corresponded with Margaret Boyle, a hostess I met on my first flight.

Knowing we could rely on the help of the airline personnel, one summer Park and I decided to fly to Miami to join a partial-sighted couple we like very much who were vacationing there. When we landed, a ground hostess was waiting to help us claim our luggage and to get us a limousine to take us to our hotel.

On our return trip my friend Charley and I were walking a little ahead of Park and Evelyn, Charley's wife, when we encountered the hostess who had helped us. "Hello, Mrs. Parker," she greeted me. "For a moment I wondered if you had exchanged husbands." After we had introduced her to our friends, she came to our assistance once more, helping us board our plane for our homeward flight.

Another amusing incident occurred on this trip. We got up early each morning to go swimming before the pool was too crowded and the sun too hot. One morning Park, Evelyn, and I left Charley in his room. A little later on hearing a noise and assuming it to be Charley, Evelyn called, "Come on in, Daddy, the water's fine."

Imagine her surprise when the owner of the hotel remarked, "You people really seem to be enjoying yourselves."

Thanks to many dedicated workers and a number of philanthropic agencies, public and private, attitudes toward the handicapped are changing, and advances resulting from technology are being made to improve their lot in life. Several bills benefiting them have been passed by both congress and state legislatures. One I consider extremely beneficial is the one which grants the blind the privilege of sending reading matter through the mail free.

Over the last few decades new methods and new appliances are being used by state schools that train visually handicapped children and rehabilitation centers that train adults with failing sight.

On a recent visit to the Kentucky School for the Blind, my Alma Mater, I was thrilled with the innovations that have taken place since I was a student there. Everything is no longer housed in one huge building. A number of smaller, attractively furnished, modern buildings are scattered over the campus. Classes are being taught in mobility, the use of the optacon—a machine which enables the blind to read printed material by touch, and in the operation of various computers.

Since I am a writer and an avid reader, I was especially impressed with the talking typewriter and the optacon. In the few minutes I was there the teacher demonstrating the optacon taught me to recognize three letters, C. S. I. A newer model of the machine, which I have not seen, is equipped with a voice box. I can see some advantages to the talking model. It should not be as difficult to master since the ear can probably transmit sounds to the brain faster than the finger can transmit images. One's reading speed should also increase. The average speed is now sixty words per minute.

The advantages of the talking typewriter are that typists can proofread their work and can check back at any time to see what they had written last.

The greatest drawback to those machines is their cost. Very few of the blind can afford them.

Of course the greatest benefit to them is the job opportunities that become available with the invention of each new machine.

Another agency helping the visually handicapped and other students with reading disabilities is Recording for the Blind, Inc. RFB is a national, voluntary, nonprofit organization which supplies free textbooks in cassette form to these students. Housed in its headquarters is a master tape library of over 55,000 books, a duplicating center, and one of the twenty-eight recording studios in the nation.

A catalog listing the titles available is distributed to schools, colleges, libraries, agencies, and individual students. Books are indexed according to authors. Recordings have been made of books in social science, applied science, mathematics, languages, technology, arts, religion, philosophy, psychology, literature, history, geography, and biography for the more than 53,000 students RFB serves.

This service is made possible by 5,000 trained volunteers who do the recording and by the generous contributions of individuals, corporations, and foundations.

Any student who cannot read printed material is eligible to borrow from RFB. The service is provided directly to each student. He registers with the agency by filling out an application for service including a signed statement by a qualified doctor, nurse, counselor, or social worker, confirming and specifying the exact nature of his handicap.

Book requests are made by mail or by calling one of RFB's toll-free numbers, 1-800-221-4792 or 1-800-221-4793. If the book is in the master tape library, it is pulled, and a copy of it is run off in the duplicating center. It is then checked by the quality control department and mailed to the student. Orders are processed and filled promptly. If the books requested are not in the library, a team of volunteers will record them in time to meet the deadlines of students served—elementary, secondary, undergraduate, graduate, and professional in all fifty states. Scholarly and complex subjects such as law, medicine, management, and so forth are read with ease and authority.

RFB welcomes qualified volunteers and donations.

Other groups throughout the country, some religious, some secular, either record or transcribe print material into braille. Some material is done for individuals. Other books are placed in a library that serves the visually handicapped. These organizations also depend on volunteers. Some of them finance their programs from individual contributions; others are funded by a specific denomination. Some religious groups prefer to have the material they supply the visually impaired recorded or brailled at one of the printing houses for the blind.

Although Southern Baptists do not have a recording studio or library for the blind, they distribute Sunday School lessons and other material through a monthly magazine. They have also published a braille edition of the Baptist Hymnal. Southern Baptists are working to promote a ministry for the blind. Cecil Ethridge has been appointed by the Home Mission Board to carry out this ministry.

In April 1982, a conference on ministries to the blind was sponsored jointly by the Sunday School Board and the Home Mission Board. Representatives from twenty-three areas of the Southern Baptist Convention were present. Two individuals from my church—Clifton Baptist Church, the Reverend Robert Williams, pastor, and Jeff Conner, minister to the visually handicapped, were invited to attend. Plans are under way to enlarge this ministry. The visually handicapped residing in some states are already receiving a taped edition of their state Baptist paper and some of the periodicals published by the Sunday School Board.

There are two national organizations of the blind, the National Federation of the Blind and the American Council of the Blind. The primary goal of these groups is to improve the social and economic well-being of the blind.

Some other agencies working in behalf of the visually handicapped are the American Foundation for the Blind, National Industries for the Blind, a Radio Information Service, and Lions International.

The American Foundation for the Blind, a private agency, is interested in all phases of blindness. It conducts surveys, promotes legislation benefiting the blind, sponsors seminars and conferences on work for the blind, grants scholarships to deserving visually handicapped students, sells aids and appliances designed to meet the needs of the sightless, and distributes material pertaining to the blind and blindness.

National Industries for the Blind procures government orders for blind-made products allocating them among the hundred or so workshops for the blind throughout the nation. These orders provide employment for approximately 5,000 visually handicapped workers.

Radio Information Service is another voluntary nonprofit agency. Volunteers read local newspapers and current magazines to visually handicapped listeners and others with reading disabilities. Special radio sets are supplied free to eligible listeners. At present more than eighty communities are being served.

Lions International is composed of Lions clubs throughout the world. Their primary goal is to aid the blind. Since 1940 my husband has been using white canes supplied by the Lions. They are doing many worthwhile things since various clubs sponsor different projects. Undoubtedly the most worthwhile is the cornea transplants made possible through Lions eye banks. Since 1958 scores of individuals have benefited from these operations. Should you wish to donate your eyes, contact your nearest Lions club for further information.

You can be one of many who care enough to lend an eye, and when you do remember our Lord's Words, "Inasmuch as ye have done it unto one of the least of these my brethren, ye have done it unto me" (Matt. 25:40).

9
Dividends of Faith

My mother was a woman of great faith. Long before I began to bombard her with questions pertaining to my blindness, she had discovered from her Bible what a friend she had in Jesus. Already she had learned to carry everything including her anguish and heartaches to him in prayer.

I'm glad and grateful Mom possessed enough faith to make prayer her first resort. I'm glad and grateful she believed in a loving God on whom one can cast every care. Because he was her friend, early in life he became my friend, too. Because she relied on the Bible and prayer for help when confronted with situations she couldn't understand, they soon became my principal sources of help also.

Over the years the seeds of faith which took root in my mind as a child have continued to grow and flourish yielding rich dividends. God's Word has remained "a lamp unto my feet, and a light unto my path" (Ps. 119:105), while prayer has always been, and still is, a vital part of my life.

Mom must have taught me to pray almost as soon as I could speak. I don't recall memorizing the childhood prayer:

> Now I lay me down to sleep,
> I pray the Lord my soul to keep;

> If I should die before I wake,
> I pray the Lord my soul to take.

Or the table grace:

> God is great, God is good,
> And we thank him for this food.

It seems as if I have known them forever.

Early in life Mom began encouraging me to say original prayers by inquiring, "Is there anything special you want to talk to Jesus about tonight?" Because of her influence, I came to regard God as the lover and keeper of my soul. The one to whom I turn whenever I feel frustrated, discouraged, or perplexed. The one I joyfully bow to when my heart overflows with thanksgiving.

In Sunday School at the little rural church my family attended, I continued to learn more about God's love for me. I remember well the Sunday School teacher I had during my childhood who really made the Bible come alive for her class. It was she who first aroused my desire to go to heaven with her beautiful portrayal of it. Midway in our lesson one of my classmates observed, "In heaven, Helen will be able to see us, won't she?"

"Indeed she will," Mrs. Grimm, our teacher, responded.

On the way home from church I informed my family that when I got to heaven I'd be able to see them and everything there. I could visualize myself as God's busiest little angel running or maybe flying to and fro gazing at all the beautiful sights. I recall thinking, *In heaven I can run as fast as I wish without bumping my head or falling down and skinning my knees.*

That night, my sister Berta dashed my hopes with her prediction that I'd probably never reach heaven. I had just said "damn" after stubbing my toe as we raced to see which of us could get to bed first.

A little later Mom found me in tears. It took some coaxing on her part to find out why I was crying. Evidently she thought my remorse sufficient punishment for the naughty word I had said. She assured me that if I were truly sorry for losing my temper God would forgive me. She taught me the following Bible verse: "If we confess our sins, he is faithful and just to forgive us our sins" (1 John 1:9). This verse and other verses of Scripture I had memorized which tell of God's love influenced my decision to want to belong to Jesus and to start living for him.

The summer I was ten, I accepted Christ as my personal Savior. I clearly remember that Thursday night in mid-July, 1925. Following the benediction, the first people to reach me were my parents. Leaning down, Dad planted a kiss on my cheek and whispered, "You'll make a wonderful little Christian."

Although Dad was a good father, a good husband, and a good neighbor, as yet he had not affiliated with any church. Since I knew a Christian should pray for and witness to lost people, I began to pray for my father. I got up early the Sunday following my conversion determined to talk to him about making a decision for Christ. He was on the front porch reading the paper. "Daddy, can I talk to you?" I asked.

"Of course," he replied. "What's on your mind?"

"Mom, my sisters, and I have been praying for you," I hurried to say before losing my courage. "Oh, Daddy, we wish you would invite Jesus to come into your heart."

He didn't answer. He just patted my hand and blew his nose.

"Are you catching cold?" I inquired.

"I don't think so," he responded. Later at church when

the visiting evangelist extended the invitation, I began to pray for my father. On the last stanza my chum interrupted my prayer to inform me, "Your dad just went forward." I could hardly wait to tell him how glad I was of his decision. When I reached him, he kissed my cheek and whispered, "Thank you, honey." We were baptized at the same time.

Several years later during a worship service, our pastor suggested that as a token of our gratitude for salvation we shake hands with the person present who had been the most instrumental in leading us to Christ. Once more Dad planted a kiss on my cheek and whispered, "Thank you, honey."

I have many fond memories of that little rural church and of my first church family. Among them were playmates I loved: Mrs. Grimm, my favorite Sunday School teacher and another dear lady who baked delicious cookies and sang the beautiful old hymns slightly off key louder than anyone else.

So many firsts occurred in my life in that little church. It was there that I first partook of the Lord's Supper and prayed in public. It was there that I experienced my first real grief at the funeral of a beloved cousin who had been my playmate, and it was there that I began to teach my first Sunday School class, a group of high school girls, some of whom were almost as old as I. I taught that class the four years I attended college.

While I was growing up, Mom assured me repeatedly that God had a definite plan for my life, that he had endowed me with the necessary talents to perfect that plan, and that if I sought his guidance he would reveal it to me. The summer following my graduation from high school, I became convinced she was absolutely right. I still consider the events of that summer miraculous.

During my junior year in high school, I was determined to attend college, if possible, even though I knew it would not be easy. The country was in the midst of the worst depression in history. My family couldn't afford to send me to college. A lack of money was by no means my only problem. Since I couldn't see, I would have to find someone to read my assignments.

Despite these obstacles Mom encouraged me not to abandon my dream. "I don't know how we'll manage it but if God wants you to go to college, he'll make it possible," she declared. "Meanwhile we'll pray and you must study hard to prepare yourself should a way be found."

The summer following my graduation, obstacle after obstacle was removed until by September they had all disappeared. In June a friend introduced me to Dr. Turck, the president of Centre College, a school within commuting distance of my home. After examining my high school record, Centre granted me a scholarship. Another friend put me in touch with a girl who would be my reader and guide in exchange for her room and board. The Division of Vocational Rehabilitation, a government agency, financed the remainder of my expenses. I even succeeded in locating a good secondhand typewriter for sale which I needed for written assignments. Luckily, I had received enough money for graduation to purchase it. In August my sister Berta obtained employment within a few blocks of Centre, thus providing Martha, my reader, and me a way to and from school. Both Martha and Lucy Anna, the two girls who helped me during college, proved to be good friends and excellent readers.

No wonder I was bubbling over with happiness and confidence the morning I stepped out of my sister's car onto the campus of Centre College. I was well on my way to becoming an English teacher. All went according to plan until my senior year at college when I learned that a blind person could not obtain a teacher's certificate in the state of Kentucky. Fortunately, this is no longer the case. Needless to say this was quite a blow since I had passed the required courses with above average grades. For a brief period I felt rejected and dejected. *What had gone wrong with my well-laid plans? Had I made a mistake to put so much faith in God? Could it be that he was not really in control of things as I had believed?* These questions nagged me briefly. My mother, who always seemed able to read my thoughts, suggested that instead of fretting about a door which had been closed that we start praying for God's guidance in finding the career he wanted me to pursue. Once more we began to pray about my future since self-pity was getting me nowhere. Once more God heard and answered our prayers. The September following my graduation from college I obtained employment as a braille proofreader for the American Printing House for the Blind in Louisville, the largest institution of its kind in the world.

As bitter as that experience had been, it taught me some important truths. I learned how essential and wise it is to pray at all times and about everything that affects one's life. I have since become aware that God's choices are far superior to mine and that heartaches and disappointments are sometimes blessings in disguise. My work as a proofreader of textbooks enabled me to help more visually handicapped students obtain an education than I could have helped had I become a teacher. Undoubtedly it also aided me in becoming a better writer, the task I enjoy most.

Once I had secured gainful employment my life became fairly routine. Like the average American woman I fell in love, married, and eventually acquired my own home. My husband and I have had the usual ups and downs. Some of them I have recounted elsewhere in this book. Satan, on numerous occasions, attempted to blind me to God's presence, love, and power, but each time God reached down to me through a passage of Scripture, or I'd recall a previous experience when he had come to my aid. Each time I turned my problem over to him he graciously supplied the extra ounce of strength, patience, faith, courage, or whatever I needed to carry on. God is so good—so exceedingly good to us when we commit our ways unto him trusting him for help.

In 1939, I transferred my letter from the Parksville Baptist Church to Clifton Baptist Church in Louisville. However, I did not become actively involved in church work until 1950. One Sunday when I taught the Sunday School lesson for a teacher who was absent, I was taken aback when a friend inquired, "Why aren't you teaching a class regularly?" Her question disturbed me. If God had endowed me with the talent to teach, should I not be making better use of it? Suddenly I realized I should be doing more for God than warming up a bench at church, dropping my offering into the collection plate on Sunday, and teaching a Sunday School class occasionally. It is amazing how God opens doors when we make our availability known to him. That week I was asked to teach one of the women's classes. Evidently I had never gotten the desire to teach completely out of my system, for this class has been a source of joy from the first Sunday I taught it.

One of my happiest memories was the Sunday morning Mom enrolled in my class. My parents moved to Louisville after Dad's retirement. I remember thinking, *For years Mom had been teaching me from God's Word. Now it is my turn to teach her, an opportunity few daughters have.* At one time my mother, my sister Daisy, and my foster sister Virgie were all in my class.

God has always stood by me in good times and bad,

amid joy and sorrow. I shall never forget a day I spent in the hospital anxiously waiting to hear the outcome of Mom's gall-bladder operation. She was eighty-three at the time of her surgery. We arrived at the hospital around 8:30 that morning. My mother was her usual calm self. Picking up her Bible she read the twenty-third Psalm aloud, then asked me to say a prayer for her recovery. I prayed two prayers simultaneously. Aloud I beseeched God to guide the surgeon and to heal my mother. Silently I implored him for strength not to give way to my emotions. He granted both requests.

I have experienced the heartbreak of saying farewell to three family members, my sister Berta, and both my parents. Words can not describe my anguish upon learning Berta had terminal cancer.

In August 1975, Dad went to be with Jesus after a heart attack. As sorry as I was to see him go, I'm grateful he didn't have to suffer and that God allowed him to attain the ripe, old age of ninety-four.

Mom was not so fortunate. Following Dad's death she insisted on maintaining her own home until she suffered a stroke eight months later. The last fifteen months of her life were miserable. She spent most of the time in hospitals or nursing homes. She never became reconciled to her physical condition. Her death in June 1977, came as a blessed relief for her.

I think the information that Mom would have to go into a nursing home caused me the most grief I have yet experienced. Telling myself that I had no other choice and that she was receiving excellent care did little to comfort me. Frequently, I left the nursing home in tears.

This continued until one evening I happened to open my Bible to these words: "In every thing give thanks: for this is the will of God in Christ Jesus concerning you" (1 Thess. 5:18).

This verse of Scripture brought me up short. Despite my unhappiness I knew I had much to be grateful for. I could and I should be giving thanks for institutions equipped to care for the aged and ailing and for the dedicated workers who minister to their needs. I could and should feel grateful for the love and concern being shown me by an understanding husband and host of wonderful friends who took me to see Mom whenever I wished to go. I was especially thankful for the enlightenment which had come to me through God's Word. Because of it, a situation which had seemed unbearable had become bearable when I was wise enough to look beyond my own grief. It was during Mom's illness that I wrote the following poem:

> Tell God when the storm clouds gather,
> And you don't know what to do;
> Trust him to supply some sunshine,
> He will always see you through.
>
> Tell God when your path is weary,
> And the way you can not see;
> Call on him for strength and guidance,
> He will always hear your plea.
>
> Tell God when your heart is aching,
> You will always find him there;
> Talk to him about your problem,
> Rest assured he'll hear your prayer.

As painful as those memories are I would not discard them if I could. I am confident they have strengthened my relationship with God.

However, the real turning point in my life came in 1974 when I learned I had to undergo back surgery. At first I refused to accept the diagnosis of the neurosurgeon who examined me.

Rather impatiently, I regret to say, I began to pray for immediate healing without an operation. I reminded God, as if I had to convince him, how busy I was. I had a home to run, a job to do, a Sunday School class to teach, and I had just accepted a brand-new assignment as program chairman of a prayer breakfast. My prayers undoubtedly sounded more like those of the spoiled child who asked God to take the vitamins out of her spinach and put them in her cake and ice cream instead of those of a committed Christian. Nevertheless, God heard and answered them not in the way I had asked but certainly in the way that was best for me. It was while I was recuperating from my operation that I finally cried out from my sickbed, "I surrender all, I surrender all; All to thee, my blessed Savior, I surrender all."

After having turned my life over to God completely, I began to search for new ways to share my faith. In addition to teaching Sunday School and planning the programs for the prayer breakfast at Clifton, I became involved in a ministry for the visually handicapped and the work of our Woman's Missionary Union there.

That same spring I met the Lucien Colemans. We became friends while Lucien was writing a feature story for *Outreach,* a Southern Baptist periodical, about my activities as a Sunday School teacher. During an interview he happened to read something I had written for our church paper. "Why don't you write an article for publication?" he inquired.

"Whatever would I write about, and who in the world would want to read it?" I exclaimed in surprise. Although I had always enjoyed jotting my thoughts down on paper I had never considered writing anything for publication. I was not yet aware I had a story to tell and the talent to tell it. However, the idea was so intriguing that I decided to accept his challenge.

I was overjoyed when the article I submitted appeared in the September 1976, issue of *Outreach*.

The previous spring I had discovered yet another way to share my faith when I accepted two speaking engagements at local Baptist churches. At one I gave my testimony; at the other I was the guest speaker for a mother-daughter banquet. My speech, a tribute to my mother, was so well received that I decided to write another article, telling how Mom had helped me accept and adjust to my handicap. That article was published in the May 1977, issue of *Home Life,* just a few weeks prior to Mom's death. She was too ill to read it, but I had read her my manuscript before mailing it.

My confidence in my ability to write was short-lived. After five rejections, I began asking myself, "Do I really possess any talent as a writer? Or is my desire to write merely a pipe dream? Should I forget it and seek other ways to serve God?" The only problem was that by then I was addicted to the extent that I didn't want to abandon my dream if there were the remotest possibility of success.

My indecision drove me to my knees. Like Gideon I needed a sign. The fleece I put out was a prayer consisting of one simple request. "Dear Lord, please show me whether or not I should continue writing."

I decided to try just once more. I submitted an article to *Outreach* about our prayer breakfast at Clifton, an activity which had become meaningful to several of us. On April 29, 1977, I learned my article had been accepted.

From then on rejections have not discouraged me because I feel I have my Lord's go-ahead signal to write.

Since my retirement in 1979, I have devoted more time to writing. Although I still free-lance, I have begun to receive assignments. My meditations have appeared in five issues of *Open Windows*. The writers conferences sponsored by the Christian Writer's Guild at the Southern Baptist Theological Seminary have helped me become better known by editors. It was at one of these conferences that Louie Wilkinson, the editor of *Adult Leadership,* suggested I compile some guidelines to help the blind and sighted relate to each other. That article, "Working with the Blind Adult," appeared in the March 1979, issue of *Adult Leadership*.

In April 1981, I was invited to Birmingham to attend a writers conference for *Royal Service* writers. This was the first curriculum I had ever done. Corresponding with missionaries serving in Spain who supplied most of the material for my assignment was exciting.

At present I am under contract to do a series of monthly articles for *Sunday School Leadership*.

Although almost all my work has appeared in Southern Baptist periodicals, some of it has been published elsewhere. Two of my meditations were printed in the *Upper Room* and a poem in *Power/Line Papers*.

While I do not enjoy speaking as much as writing, I seldom decline an invitation to speak if I can fit it into my schedule. I have spoken to Dr. Coleman's Christian writing classes at Southern Seminary, at banquets and retreats, and to women's groups and senior citizens' groups. In October 1980, I was privileged to plan and lead a retreat for pastors' wives in southern Indiana. The theme was "Reach Out to Christ and for Christ."

Although I regard my ability to write and speak as a means of witnessing, it has brought me some recognition. Articles have been written about my activities for the Baptist Press, *Royal Service,* and the *Western Recorder,* Kentucky's Baptist paper.

October 26, 1980, was designated as Visually Handicapped Day at my church. I was on the committee to recommend some of the people to be recognized. I had no idea I was to be one of them. That morning much to my surprise I was one of the recipients to receive a certificate of appreciation. I am extremely grateful to my pastor, the Reverend Robert Williams, for including me.

Another pleasant surprise that has come my way is the scores of fan letters I have received from people of all ages and from every walk of life. Letters have come from a missionary couple in Africa, a former pastor in Canada, from students, homemakers, professional people, and senior citizens. One letter arrived from a hospital room, one from prison, another from a nine-year-old girl; two were in braille, and two were from former members of the Sunday School class I taught while attending college. Some of my readers were facing crises, others wrote to express their appreciation of my work and to urge me to continue writing. The majority of them claimed they had been helped, blessed, and inspired by my work.

Whatever their reasons for contacting me, I am grateful to God for the opportunity to help them. My prayer is that as long as I write, my words will point them to a loving God who gives hope to a despairing soul, peace to a troubled heart, and light for a dark day.

In October 1981, while doing my laundry, I fell in my basement and broke my hip. Despite the fact that I was confined to my bedroom for three months my faith never wavered. I managed to stay happy and to continue witnessing. God really blessed me through wonderful friends, many of whom were members of my church family. They brightened my days with their cards, telephone calls, prayers, visits, and other deeds of kindness. I received over two hundred get-well cards. I had enough writing and church work to keep me busy. The only task I relinquished was teaching my Sunday School class since I couldn't figure out a way to do it, and since Daisy volunteered to teach for me. I narrated the programs for our prayer breakfast by means of a cassette tape. I planned the programs for the Week of Prayer and promoted our Foreign and Home Mission Board offerings. I was able to meet all my deadlines for the assignments I had accepted.

One of the first services I attended when my doctor dismissed me was the March prayer breakfast. Jackie Powell, one of the committee members, had prepared a big sign extending across the front of the fellowship hall which said, "Welcome back, Helen, we love you." The display of such affection left me feeling proud yet humble.

Now that I am back on my feet again my supreme desire is to serve God wherever I can, in all the ways that I can, as well as I can, and for as long as I can. The following prayer which I wrote shortly after my retirement expresses my feelings. It is a prayer I have prayed often since then:

Lord, thank you for allowing me to reach another milestone in life, my retirement. I am aware, Father, I shall have to make some adjustments. But with your leadership and guidance retirement should present no real problem. Actually, I can already perceive some advantages: fewer pressures, more time and opportunities for Bible study, prayer, and Christian service. After all, Lord, I've just retired from a paying job and not from serving you. And so I pray that you will continue to make my life useful to you.

Should I be called to some difficult or unpleasant task help me not to hide behind the excuse "I'm getting too old. Perhaps you'd better get somebody else." However, Father, when the time eventually comes that I can no longer serve in certain areas help me to step aside gracefully. But, even then, Father, may I never lose sight of your fields white unto harvest. May I never cease praying for the laborers who will replace me.

In Christ's name, hear my prayer. Amen.

10
Life Can Be Beautiful

Some of my close friends who may be a bit prejudiced, bless their hearts, consider me a success. It is not because of fame, fortune, power, or prestige, for alas! I have acquired none of these. *Then why do they consider you a success?* I can almost hear you asking. One only plausible explanation I can come up with is that it must be my philosophy of life. I am thoroughly convinced, and one of my goals is to convince others through my writing, speaking, and teaching, that life can be beautiful regardless of one's circumstances.

You don't have to be born with a silver spoon in your mouth. I wasn't, and yet I was a happy child who liked to laugh and play. A favorite childhood pastime of mine was dressing up in Mom's high-heeled shoes and pretending to be some outstanding personality. At times I was a beautiful princess; at other times a famous movie star; always I was a great lady.

I could hardly wait until I was old enough to have a pair of high-heeled shoes of my own. I distinctly remember the first pair my parents purchased for me. I was so proud of them. Putting them on I paraded around the house thinking all the while, *I'm almost as tall as Mom and my sisters.*

I decided I'd wear them back to school. Although not accustomed to wearing high heels, I got along fine until I started my descent from the train. Somehow I caught my heel on the top step. I would have fallen flat on my face had I not been holding onto the arm of the porter. Thanks to his strong arm and my tight grip onto it I managed to reach the station platform upright but minus the heel from one of my beautiful new shoes. I was too embarrassed to acknowledge my loss. Saying nothing I started through the station walking on my toes. I had taken only a few steps when someone tapped me on the shoulder. "Pardon me, but isn't this your heel?" a stranger inquired.

I had to admit that it was. Heel in hand and with cheeks stinging, I proceeded on my way. When I arrived at school a short time later, still clutching my heel, my friends who were already there greeted me warmly.

As commonplace and ordinary as that experience was, it helped me discover it isn't what we wear but who we are that makes us stand tall. Zacchaeus, the chief tax collector of Jericho, was a little man, small in stature and in spirit until he met Jesus. From that day on he was never the same. One never is. Christ adds beauty, meaning, and purpose to life. Without him we are nothing. Without him we soon lose faith in God, humanity, and ourselves. Without him we could never reach heaven.

At the age of ten I discovered I didn't have to go through life without Christ. Having him as my Lord and Savior has made a difference in the way I think, speak, and act. Knowing how much he loved me has helped me love and accept others. Becoming aware of how he ministered to the less fortunate has made it easier for me to help them. Knowing he was victorious over his enemies has given me new hope. With Christ as my example, like Zacchaeus, I shall never be the same. He has shown me how special I am to God.

I am reminded of this each time I look at a beautiful

ceramic vase I received as a gift sometime ago. On it are stamped these words: "What I am is my gift from God; what I become is my gift to him." I have truly come to believe that my life is a priceless gift designed exclusively for me and no one else by a loving, Heavenly Father.

Therefore, I should use my time, talents, energy, training, and possessions in such a way that my life shapes up according to God's design for it. Because I am a unique individual, a special somebody in his sight, I should strive to make my life as beautiful and worthwhile as he, the master designer, and I working together can possibly make it.

I believe some ways I can do this are to use my blindness as a stepping stone rather than as a stumbling block and to brighten the corner wherever I am. In order to attain these goals I must remember that life is too short and too precious to be squandered or hidden away. If my life is to be beautiful, I cannot afford to waste it in selfish pursuits or to let it pass me by. I must take advantage of every opportunity to live joyfully and fully by saying yes to the things that will bring lasting happiness and no to those things that will bring regret. By so doing I shall store up pleasant memories for my twilight hours. Then when the clock of life starts winding down, I shall be able to say, "Life has been beautiful. I have experienced true happiness."

Happiness comes not from what one gets but from what one gives; not from what one says he believes but from how he lives; not from how others regard him but from how he regards them; not from discarding God's plan for his life but from a daily walk with him.

God is no far-off presence in some distant land. He is the Christian's constant companion, surrounding him with matchless love; upholding him with his outstretched arms; walking beside him lest he stumble and fall; reaching out to him in his time of need; and abiding within him to empower him for the task ahead.

But God is like any other friend. The more time we spend in his company listening to what he has to say to us in his Word and talking to him in prayer, the better we will get to know him. The closer we stay to him on our journey through life the more our friendship with him will grow. He wants to be our friend.

God is such a faithful friend. He never closes one door without opening another. He never asks us to bear a heavier cross than the one he bore. And he never deprives us of one blessing without bestowing another. For example, I did not receive sight, but I was given insight. God is mindful of our needs whether material or spiritual, few or many, great or small. Oh, how he loves you and me!

No matter what we do he never stops loving us. We cannot prevent God from shedding his love abroad any more than we can prevent the sun from shining. The sun continues to shine even when its rays are shut out of a house with drawn blinds. God continues to love mankind even though some individuals try to crowd his love out of their lives. His love is everlasting; his mercy endures forever.

From the time of creation he has been blessing mankind in many wonderful ways. Not only did he give him the dominion over everything on earth, but he has given him the strength and skill to subdue it. As if that were not enough, he sent his own dear Son to earth that we might have eternal life. And even now he is preparing a permanent dwelling place in heaven for our future abode. Such love and generosity are beyond human comprehension.

This is good to know since there are such few things in life on which we can depend. We can't depend on the weather because it changes constantly. We can't depend on people because sometimes they forsake us. Nor can we depend on life itself, for it can be snuffed out in an instant. However, we can always depend on God. Great is his faithfulness.

He is the same yesterday, today, and forever. His power will never decrease, nor his love for his children wax cold. Man sometimes thwarts God's plans, but he cannot defeat his purpose. God remains in control of the universe, bringing order out of chaos. He continues to work in every situation bringing victory out of defeat for those who trust him.

Reflect for just a moment on how often good things result from something seemingly bad. Take Good Friday, for example. On that dreadful day, stunned and shocked, our Lord's disciples wondered, *What are we to do now?*

We will have days similar to that. Days on which our hopes are dashed, our dreams shattered, and our faith shakened. And yet, without Good Friday there would have been no Easter.

The statement "April showers bring May flowers" does little to comfort us when a rainy day spoils our plans unless we learn to look beyond the showers for the flowers that come later. Those who concentrate on the showers forgetting the flowers lose sight of an important truth. Without the one there would not be the other, God's reason for sending both sunshine and rain.

As the poet declared, "God has not promised skies always blue." We can expect certain obstacles. The secret of overcoming them is to believe that God will not permit any obstacle to block your path that he and you pulling together cannot surmount, and to develop an I'm-going-to-make-it-regardless-of attitude. Armed with that kind of faith and that sort of attitude no obstacle will ever be big enough to keep you down. Total deafness did not stop

Beethoven from composing his ninth symphony, nor did the loss of sight cause Milton to lay aside his pen.

So, no matter how dreary your present or how stormy your past, your future can be bright if you will trust God enough to rely on his promises. He never made a single promise that he cannot and will not keep. His promises are everlasting, and they were meant for you and me. Someone has compared them to chimes in the night, vibrating with God's love and faithfulness. As we listen to their joyful sounds, why not resolve to let their message of hope penetrate our hearts and dispel our gloom?

Some of his promises which I have hidden in my heart that are beautifying my life follow:

"Call unto me, and I will answer thee, and shew thee great and mighty things, which thou knowest not" (Jer. 33:3).

"The effectual fervent prayer of a righteous man availeth much" (Jas. 5:16).

"Fear thou not; for I am with thee: be not dismayed; for I am thy God: I will strengthen thee; yea, I will help thee; yea, I will uphold thee with the right hand of my righteousness" (Isa. 41:10).

"God is our refuge and strength, a very present help in trouble" (Ps. 46:1).

"In all thy ways acknowledge him, and he shall direct thy paths" (Prov. 3:6).

"There hath no temptation taken you but such as is common to man: but God is faithful, who will not suffer you to be tempted above that ye are able; but will with the temptation also make a way to escape, that ye may be able to bear it" (1 Cor. 10:13).

"For I am persuaded, that neither death, nor life, nor angels, nor principalities, nor powers, nor things present, nor things to come, Nor height, nor depth, nor any other creature, shall be able to separate us from the love of God, which is in Christ Jesus our Lord" (Rom. 8:38-39).

"But my God shall supply all your need according to his riches in glory by Christ Jesus" (Phil. 4:19).

"Lo, I am with you alway, even unto the end of the world" (Matt. 28:20).

In addition to these and other marvelous promises God has given us another priceless gift, the gift of prayer:

> God knew the sun would not always shine,
> Some days would be bleak and gray,
> He knew of our need for faith and hope,
> So he taught us how to pray.
>
> God knew that into each life would come
> Some sorrow, some stress and care,
> So to help us cope, he gave to us
> The wonderful gift of prayer.
>
> How reassuring it is to know
> Our Heavenly Father's there
> To watch over us, supply our needs,
> And listen to every prayer.

Writing program material for a prayer breakfast at my church has given me the opportunity to share this gift with others. At one of the programs each person received a booklet containing the following prayer suggestions:

It is my prayer that these suggestions will help you pray more effectively, truly worship, and live more victoriously.

1. To better attain these goals, study God's Word prayerfully.
2. As you pray, picture God as your Creator and Redeemer.

3. Spend some time in prayer alone with God each day.
4. Begin and end each day in prayer.
5. Say grace before each meal.
6. Send up flash prayers to God night or day.
7. Put aside every distracting thought.
8. Ask God to remove all your worry and tension.
9. If fears and doubts assail you, entreat God to dispel them.
10. Be still mentally, so that you can feel God's presence and guidance.
11. Don't just go through the motions of prayer. Concentrate on talking to God.
12. Don't pray to impress men.
13. Make your prayers a form of worship as well as a list of requests.
14. Always pray reverently and humbly.
15. Pray intelligently. Don't attempt to bargain with God.
16. Seek God's will for your life, even if it conflicts with your desires.
17. Always pray in the name of Jesus.
18. Don't hesitate to claim God's promises.
19. Expect God to hear and answer your prayers.
20. If your prayers are not answered immediately, continue praying.
21. Whenever your prayers are not answered in the way you expect, remember this: "And we know that all things work together for good to them that love God" (Rom. 8:28*a*).
22. Occasionally, you may not know how to pray. At such times, trust the Holy Spirit to intercede in your behalf.
23. Never be embarrassed about letting others know how much you rely on prayer.

24. When seeking help, make prayer your first, not your last, resort.
25. Be honest in your prayers of confession. God can be trusted to forgive.
26. Mention specific sins such as malice, pride, and envy that you need help in overcoming.
27. Ask God to deliver you from temptation.
28. Seek God's guidance before making decisions.
29. Invite Jesus to come into your heart and to take complete possession of your life.
30. Pray to become a good steward of your time, talents, and possessions.
31. Seek God's guidance in discovering the particular task he has for you.
32. Ask God that the fruit of the Spirit may be evident in your daily life.
33. Pray that you may be clothed in the armor of God.
34. Pray that your faith will not waver.
35. Pray for the work of the church and the advancement of God's kingdom.
36. Pray for our country and all who hold positions of leadership.
37. Remember others in your prayers.
38. Take time to pray with a friend in trouble.
39. Identify with those for whom you pray.
40. Have a prayer list calling by name those you are concerned about.
41. Make specific prayer requests, such as: "Give us this day our daily bread" (Matt. 6:11).
42. If you are getting neither the satisfaction nor the results from your prayers you feel you should, like the disciples, ask Jesus to instruct you.
43. Thank God for answered prayer.
44. Praise God from whom all blessings flow.

45. Give thanks for God's unfailing love.
46. Be especially thankful to God for the gift of his Son despite our unworthiness.
47. Pray that you may be more worthy of God's love.
48. Thank God for giving you another chance.
49. Ask God to help you to turn your thanksgiving into "thanksliving."
50. My final suggestion was the prayer of a country parson: "God, fill my mouth with worthwhile stuff, but nudge me when I've said enough."

Other groups have used these suggestions. One group used them at a prayer retreat. A friend used them for a prayer breakfast at her church.

As we pray let's remember that God's storehouse in heaven is full of rare treasures he wants to bestow on us.

Ask, expecting to receive; seek, expecting to find; knock, believing that he will open up his treasure chests. Prayer is the flood gates that open heaven allowing God's blessings to flow down to us. When Elijah and Hannah prayed, requests that had seemed impossible were granted.

Of course, God answers prayers in various ways. Sometimes the answer is yes. At other times it is no or wait. If the answer is yes, accept it gladly and gratefully. Should it be no or wait, don't make the mistake of doubting God's love for you or of thinking your prayers have gone unheard. Remember his timing and man's timing are not necessarily the same. Continue in prayer, confident that each one will be answered at the right time and in the right way. Our Heavenly Father hears them all whether long or short, spoken or unspoken. How fortunate we are that he never sleeps, he never goes on vacation, and he is never beyond our reach.

Consequently, no time is as well spent as the time we

spend in Bible study, in prayer, and in sharing God's love
with others. A day without reading the Bible is like going
on a journey without a road map. A day without prayer is
a lost opportunity to talk to God. A day without sharing
God's love with someone cheats him and us of a blessing
God wants to bestow through us.

Our Lord has given us many gifts to share—gifts that
require no special training, and yet they are more valuable than silver and gold. A cheery smile, some words of
encouragement or praise, some little acts of kindness,
and the privilege of praying one for another are just a few
of them. He also gives us many opportunities to share
these gifts. Don't underestimate them even though they
seem small and unimportant to you. Anything we can do
for the Lord is worth doing, and nothing we do in his
name escapes his notice. Furthermore, I dare to say it is
the little things we often take for granted that bring us
the most happiness. They also remind us how good God is
to provide each of us the kind of help we need.

To those without sight God gives the ability to hear the
friendly hello or the generous offer of help from a
concerned bystander. To those who cannot hear or speak
he gives the warm smile or the outstretched hand of
caring individuals to assure them of his care. To all of
mankind who will accept it he gives cleansing and
pardon, and to make life a little more beautiful he gives
yet another gift—a grateful heart for his love and mercy.

How long has it been since you counted your blessings?
Recently each time I have tried to count mine, my list
grew longer and longer until I realized how impossible it
is. God keeps blessings upon us day after day whether or
not we are aware of him and them.

Counting blessings is the best remedy I have found for
curing the blues, and it is a much better way to spend a
sleepless night than counting sheep. As I name my

blessings one by one, I'm always surprised at what the Lord has done for me, and sometimes I'm a little ashamed of my ingratitude. Whenever that occurs I say this prayer, the opening line of a poem: "Lord, forgive me when I whine."

Another gift I consider priceless is that of friendship. For years, Lorene Edds, a dear friend, has helped me. Other members of my church family read to me and assist me in countless ways. A former braille transcriber, Mattie Ragsdale, transcribes material into braille for the visually handicapped who attend Clifton. Mae Sympson, a member of my Sunday School class, wrote the following tribute to me:

So many tributes are paid to so many people, usually those well known to the public, movie stars, etc. I would like to pay tribute to a Sunday School teacher whom I have known for many years and have sat under her teaching for the past three years at least. I'm talking about a small person, in stature that is, soft of voice and gentle in manner, yet, what a dynamic person she is. Her fingers fly over her pages; yes, she is reading braille, while her tongue does a fantastic job of keeping up! She has a wonderful way with words, never faltering for the right one which always seems to be at her "finger's tip."

She is rather quiet, yet her presence is felt the moment she enters a room. How such a petite person can fill the largest room is beyond comprehension. Yet, is it? Her sense of humor, her ready laugh, her love and concern for everybody, her understanding of human problems and perplexities all go to make up this sweet Christian character.

I have always been a great admirer of Fanny Crosby, who wrote so many of our beautiful hymns. I know that when I reach heaven, she will be one of the first persons I will want to meet and thank. Somehow as I think of her and meditate on the beautiful hymns she has written, the person who flashes before my eyes is my Sunday School teacher. A much younger person to be sure, and a much younger person than any of the ladies in her class, yet they look to her Sunday after Sunday with great anticipation for a lesson brought after careful and prayerful preparation which is always a message for each heart and a blessing for each life. I know that she would that we never see her nor hear her, but that we would see and hear the Christ whom she presents to us.

She is a busy person, yet she is never too busy to stop and to listen when one has a question or a problem, and somehow, she seems to hold the key that unlocks the door to the answers and clarifies the mysteries which are of great concern to those who seek her counsel.

I cannot present her with an Oscar or an Emmy, but I can pay this tribute to her and hold fast to the hope that she will have a long and fruitful life, and that many more will have the privilege of sitting under her teaching and being touched by her life.

"Every word was from my heart," Mae's response to my accusation that her praise had been too extravagant, brought tears to my eyes.

Still another priceless gift which enhances the beauty of life is freedom of choice. By using this gift wisely and well I can become what God created me to be, saved me to be, and has called me to be.

When I fail, I can ask God to pick me up and give me the courage to keep trying. I don't have to be a drop-out.

I can be open and receptive to the lessons my Lord would teach me through daily experiences. I can request him to keep me aware that life is a time of striving; a time for learning and growing; a time of going forward. It is never at a standstill, and few things are ever learned in one easy lesson.

I can count on God's guidance in attaining the goals I set for myself. If I wish to have friends, I must choose to be a friend. If I desire love, I must choose to show love. If I want my life to be Christ centered I must allow Christ to dwell within me. Whatever my goals, I must choose to trust God, think big, dream big, and work hard.

I must choose all ways to give God my best. Surely the giver of so many and such good and perfect gifts deserves my best. I dare not attempt to satisfy him with my left-overs. I dare not presume to honor him with less than the best. I am aware the gift he considers best and desires most is first place in my life. I have chosen to offer him this gift wholeheartedly with no strings attached.

Frequently I tell my audiences, "The secret of my success is that I stay much too busy, I'm far too optimistic, and I'd like to think too intelligent to waste valuable time indulging in self-pity or fretting about situations that cannot be altered. When tempted to feel sorry for myself or to get upset over talents I do not possess or things I cannot do, I remember that Mary was only a peasant girl and Joseph the village carpenter. Yet God used them to turn the tide of history."

I must never forget that fear blinds me to God's presence and power in my life; faith opens my eyes, heart, and mind not only to his presence and power but to his love and grace as well. Fear paralyzes me filling me with self-doubt, faith releases me to overcome the enemies that would subdue me. Fear diminishes the joy of my salvation; faith assures me of victory in Jesus. When tempted to fear, I can pray, "Replace my fear with faith, dear Father."

Since I rely on God's leadership, I can go where he beckons unafraid; I can climb mountains or pass through valleys even though the road is rough and the way unfamiliar. I can journey on amid sunshine or rain, joy or sorrow until I reach my destination. Some may regard my trail as a dark one, but I disagree because Jesus is the light of my life and I have learned to walk by faith and not by sight.

Where to Go for Help

Rehabilitation Services
  Administration
Office for the Blind and Visually
  Handicapped
330 C Street, S.W.
Washington, DC 20201
(202) 245-0918

National Institutes of Health
National Eye Institute
Bethesda, MD 20014
(301) 496-2234

Library of Congress
Division for the Blind and
  Physically Handicapped
1291 Taylor Street, N.W.
Washington, DC 20542
(202) 882-5500

Eye-Bank Association of
  America, Inc.
3195 Maplewood Avenue
Winston-Salem, NC 27103
(919) 768-0719

American Council of the Blind,
  Inc.
501 North Douglas Avenue
Oklahoma City, OK 73106
(405) 232-4644

American Federation of Catholic
  Workers for the Blind and
  Visually Handicapped, Inc.

154 East Twenty-third Street
New York, NY 10010

The Association of Junior
  Leagues, Inc.
825 Third Avenue
New York, NY 10022
(212) 355-4380

Blinded Veterans Association
1735 DeSales Street, N.W.
Washington, DC 20036
(202) 347-4010

Delta Gamma Foundation
6940 West Floyd Avenue
Lakewood, CO 80227

Episcopal Guild for the Blind
157 Montague Street
Brooklyn, NY 11201
(212) 625-4886

The International Association of
  Lions Clubs
300 Twenty-second Street
Oak Brook, IL 60521
(312) 986-1700

Louis Braille Foundation for
  Blind Musicians, Inc.
215 Park Avenue South
New York, NY 10003
(212) 982-7290

National Federation of the Blind
1800 Johnson Street
Baltimore, MD 21230
(301) 659-9314

Fight for Sight, Inc.
National Council to Combat
  Blindness, Inc.
41 West Fifty-seventh Street
New York, NY 10019
(212) 751-1118

Research to Prevent Blindness,
  Inc.
598 Madison Avenue
New York, NY 10022
(212) 752-4333

American Foundation for the
  Blind, Inc.
15 West Sixteenth Street
New York, NY 10011
(212) 620-2000

National Society for the
  Prevention of Blindness
79 Madison Avenue
New York, NY 10016
(212) 684-3505

American Bible Society
1865 Broadway
New York, NY 10023
(212) 581-7400

American Printing House for the
  Blind, Inc.
1839 Frankfort Avenue
Louisville, KY 40206
(502) 895-2405

Braille Circulating Library
2700 Stuart Avenue
Richmond, VA 23220
(804) 359-3743

The Braille Evangel, Inc.
P.O. Box 6399
Fort Worth, TX 76115
(817) 923-0603

Braille Institute of America, Inc.
741 North Vermont Avenue
Los Angeles, CA 90029
(213) 663-1111

Choice Magazine Listening
14 Maple Street
Port Washington, NY 11050
(516) 883-8280

Christian Mission for the
  Sightless
Rural Route 1
New Ross, IN 47968
(317) 723-1613

Christian Record Braille
  Foundation, Inc.
4444 South Fifty-second Street
Lincoln, NB 68506
(402) 488-0981

Clovernook Printing House for
  the Blind
7000 Hamilton Avenue
Cincinnati, OH 45231
(513) 522-3860

Dialogue Publications, Inc.
3100 Oak Park Avenue
Berwyn, IL 60402
(312) 749-1908/1909

Gospel Association for the Blind,
  Inc.
15-16 College Point Boulevard
College Point, NY 11356
(212) 353-7577

Hadley School for the Blind
700 Elm Street
Winnetka, IL 60093
(312) 446-8111

Howe Press of Perkins School for
the Blind
175 North Beacon Street
Watertown, MA 02172
(617) 924-3434

Jewish Braille Institute of
America, Inc.
110 East Thirtieth Street
New York, NY 10016
(212) 889-2525

John Milton Society for the
Blind
29 West Thirty-fourth Street, 6th
Floor
New York, NY 10001
(212) 736-4162

Lutheran Braille Workers, Inc.
11735 Peach Tree Circle
Yucaipa, CA 92399
(714) 797-3093

Lutheran Library for the Blind
3558 South Jefferson Avenue
Saint Louis, MO 63118
(314) 664-7000, Ext. 388

Matilda Ziegler Magazine for the
Blind
20 West Seventeenth Street
New York, NY 10011
(212) 242-0263

National Association for
Visually Handicapped, Inc.
305 East Twenty-fourth Street
New York, NY 10010
(212) 889-3141

National Braille Association
654A Godwin Avenue
Midland Park, NJ 07432
(201) 447-1484

National Braille Press, Inc.
88 Saint Stephen Street
Boston, MA 02115
(617) 366-6750

Recording for the Blind, Inc.
215 East Fifty-eighth Street
New York, NY 10022
(212) 751-0860

Volunteer Services for the Blind,
Inc.
919 Walnut Street
Philadelphia, PA 19107
(215) 627-0600

Xavier Society for the Blind
154 East Twenty-third Street
New York, NY 10010
(212) 473-7800